Michael Sadler once wrote a doctoral thesis on the failure of the French Symbolist poets to write fiction. He has since managed marginally better himself. His work includes writing for BBC Radio 3 and television, a history of music in strip cartoons, a French art-house film starring Jean-Louis Trintignant and translations of Marivaux for the BBC/RSC. He teaches French at the British Institute in Paris where he runs an MA course in Contemporary French Studies. He likes Schubert, Led Zeppelin and, if he ever had the chance to taste it, Château Pétrus. He lives in Paris and the Touraine. He has a French wife, a French–English daughter and grows his own leeks.

An Englishman in Paris

L'éducation continentale

Michael Sadler

POCKET
BOOKS

LONDON · SYDNEY · NEW YORK · TOKYO · SINGAPORE · TORONTO

First published in Great Britain in 2002
by Simon & Schuster UK Ltd
This edition published in 2003 by Pocket Books
A Viacom company

First published in France in 2000
as *Un Anglais à Paris* by L'Archipel

5 7 9 10 8 6 4

Simon & Schuster UK Ltd
Africa House
64–78 Kingsway
London WC2B 6AH

Simon & Schuster Australia
Sydney

A CIP catalogue record for this book is available from the
British Library

ISBN 0-7434-4046-3

Typeset in Sabon by Palimpsest Book Production Limited,
Polmont, Stirlingshire
Printed and bound in Great Britain by
Cox & Wyman Ltd, Reading, Berkshire

For Lulu and Daisy

Preface

by Peter Mayle

Sadler was born in Lewes, a small town in the south of England. This was a geographical accident. He should have emerged from the womb in Paris, looking anxiously about him for a suitable place to have lunch.

I have never met an Englishman who is so thoroughly French. His appearance, the inflections of his speech, the constant waggle of his hands, eyebrows and shoulders, his perfectly formed Gallic pout, even the way he approaches a glass of Côtes-du-Rhône – all these are much more at home in Saint-Germain than they could ever be in Sussex.

Sadler shares with the French a deep and abiding concern for the stomach, a delight in food and wine that is evident in a variety of ways. There is, for instance, the selection of photographs he keeps in the pocket next to his heart. Other men carry around pictures of their loved ones – wives, children, occasionally dogs or parrots – which they will bring out to show you with the kind of modest pride reserved for favoured possessions. Sadler's prized photographs vary with the seasons: potatoes, leeks and tomatoes, still-life studies of the produce he grows in his country garden in Touraine.

This is a man who has persuaded his friend Goujon the butcher to supply him with made-to-measure sausages of a specific length, circumference and spiciness. If you should ask what makes them superior to the standard-issue sausage, you will be treated to a lecture – in between meals, Sadler is a university professor – and the lecture will cover, in considerable detail, the anatomy of the sausage from skin to stuffing before moving on to cooking techniques, recipes and one or two appropriate wines. Other subjects in the curriculum include tripe, cheese (with a special tutorial on Livarot, where Sadler is a member of the cheese peerage), fish, bread and pigs' ears.

Another of his abiding passions is Paris. In particular, the 6th *arrondissement*, where he lives, happily surrounded by butchers, bakers, pastry cooks, fishmongers, restaurants, wine *caves* and *traiteurs*. Here, the perfumes of food escape through open doorways, lingering seductively in the streets. The neighbourhood is a dieter's nightmare, relieved only by the odd pharmacy providing tonics for a faltering digestion and remedies for an overstressed liver.

After many years of enthusiastic research, Sadler has gathered around him a group of local *fournisseurs* – all within a short stroll of his apartment – who help him keep body and soul together. These are dedicated men, the kind of men you can trust with your stomach. Over time, they have become friends. And, one drizzly March morning, I was taken to meet some of them.

In the course of a couple of hours, I was introduced to Dédé l'Asperge and his wife Gilberte, who run the café Le Balto. To Goujon the butcher, and to Didier the fishmonger. You will find them lovingly described in the pages that follow. But, for reasons of modesty or perhaps a latent twinge of Anglo-Saxon embarrassment, the author doesn't describe the obvious fondness that these unsentimental Parisians feel for their English *copain*. It first shows itself in an extensive physical ritual. Kisses, many kisses, are exchanged. Cheeks are pinched, backs rubbed, shoulders gripped, kidneys patted. Once an inventory of the major organs has been completed, conversation can begin. This too is punctuated by tweaks and squeezes and the occasional bout of massage.

It is not long before food is discussed, and fingers fondle the air as a particularly voluptuous recipe is explained and illustrated. Prime cuts of meat, trays of hand-made sausages, a gleaming sea bass – these are brought out and presented for inspection, in the manner of a fond parent introducing a handsome and gifted child.

Eventually, as noon approaches, I feel sure I can hear a low, persistent sound coming from somewhere beneath Sadler's raincoat. It is the discreet rumbling of a stomach that is ready for lunch.

This had been planned weeks before in the course of several long telephone calls; lunch, in Sadler's view, being far too serious a matter to be left to chance. We had finally decided to try the restaurant of Hélène Darroze in the rue d'Assas. One Michelin star, and an impressive reputation, even among blasé Parisians, for the kind of cooking that brings tears of pleasure to a strong man's eyes. The perfect setting, we told one another, in which to discuss the social and cultural aspects of Sadler's book, the different challenges of writing it, as he had done, in both French and English, the role of the memoir in contemporary literature, and anything else that would enable me to write a suitably thoughtful and scholarly preface.

Alas, our good intentions were no match for the cuisine of Madame Darroze. I'm afraid we allowed ourselves to be distracted. There was the menu to inspect, then the wine list. And then, just as we were about to get to grips with the influence of Proust and the use of the interior mono-logue, we were interrupted by platefuls of baby asparagus, which prompted Sadler to mutter to the waiter about *une tendresse extraordinaire*; next, lightly cooked *foie gras* with a chutney made from tropical fruits, followed by perfectly aged cheeses, and a dessert of unimaginable delicacy. All of these, of course, had to be given their due attention. We suddenly realized that two hours had gone by, and we had talked of nothing but food. The death blow to any remaining

hopes of literary cut-and-thrust was delivered at the end of
the meal, when the waiter wheeled up a trolley of vintage
Armagnacs (1939 was a spectacularly good year).

So much for the scholarly preface. Luckily, this is a
book that explains itself with wit and affection as it goes
along, pausing frequently for nourishment, or to muse on
the advantages of understanding cricket when romantically
involved with a Frenchwoman. But most of all, it is a love
letter to Paris and some of the people of Paris. And, like all
the best love letters, it leaves the reader wanting more.

                                        Peter Mayle, 2002

1

The Englishman looked at the cheese and the cheese looked at the Englishman.

The Englishman was me. The cheese – soft, fat, orange and too big for its box; a rubicund monk against a backdrop of smiling cows – was a Livarot. We were both in Dieppe high street. The cheese was in a glass case, me in my summer suit. The cheese knew I was just off the ferry. It knew I wanted it. If a cheese can be a turn-on, this one was very sexy.

I've never had a Livarot of my own. I'd often given them surreptitious glances as they lounged voluptuously on the marble slabs of shady *crémeries* but, until now, I'd always managed to rein in my enthusiasm with arguments such as: 1, they stink; 2, you can die of them. But today, if I wanted to, I could. *Pourquoi pas?*

I was going to learn my lesson the hard way. Buying a Livarot is one thing; living with one is another kettle of fish. I opened the door of the *épicerie fine*. The proprietor in his long white apron oozed out from the back of the shop where he'd probably been spending the morning humming Georges Brassens to the inmates. He was like his cheeses: large, ripe, and at least 60 per cent fat.

'*Je voudrais un Livarot*, please,' I managed to dribble.

'*Un colonel, monsieur?*'

'*Excusez-moi?*'

Livarots, he explained, come in various sizes: S, M, L, XL and, the largest of them all, the *colonel* – the rank indicated by five green strands of raffia tied around his waist like a cummerbund on a Welsh baritone.

'*Je prends le colonel, s'il vous plaît.*'

A whole brigade were brought out on parade, squeezed and lifted to the nose. The victim was selected and required a shoe-horn to be returned to its box. I was now the proud owner of a pungent amber pouffe made from at least five litres of curdled milk. I left the *épicerie*, my heart beating fast.

I walked down the high street towards the port. Dieppe has changed a lot. The boat from Newhaven no longer docks in the centre of the town, and the enormous ugly concrete construction which housed the customs and the *gare maritime* has been destroyed to reveal a very beautiful *quai* of old buildings now running along what has become a harbour for smart yachts. Along the quayside were a string of restaurants offering what I called – my first French joke – *la cuisine d'Allah*: *moules allah crème, sole allah normande* etc. It all looked like a tourist's dream. If the town council hadn't come up with the bright idea of slipping an ugly black asphalt car park between the restaurants and the port, the whole place was in grave danger of becoming chic. Dieppe happily remains Dieppe. It was a close shave.

Sitting on the *terrasse* of the Tout Va Bien with a crisp, cool, springlike glass of sauvignon, I was taken with the desire to sink my teeth into the colonel's buttocks. Being rather self-conscious, and never having seen anyone eat a Livarot in the street with his fingers, I compromised. I took a sip of the wine and lifted the plastic bag to my nose for a quick whiff. The children at a nearby table eyed the newly arrived pervert with interest.

'*Pourquoi le monsieur renifle son sac, papa?*'

To dispel any suspicion, I ordered a *bouillabaisse dieppoise*, a bottle of *gros plant* and sat the colonel down opposite me. We had lunch together. This gave me time to peruse the instruction booklet which came with the cheese. The Livarot, a speciality of the Pays d'Auge, is encased in its belt of rushes to stop it sinking back into itself. These greenish strands are called *laiches*. I jotted it down. A rush hernia belt for cheese is not the world's most useful word, but if you're going to learn the language, you've got to start somewhere. The Livarot was highly regarded as early as the thirteenth century and was France's favourite in the nineteenth. There was none on the menu so I wound up with a *flan aux pruneaux* and, purely for medicinal purposes, *un petit calva* – a very effective mouthwash.

About three o'clock we decided to hit the road.

It was round about Tôtes, about twenty kilometres from Dieppe, that the military gentleman on the back seat of the Mazda began to make his presence felt. Maybe he'd caught the sun during lunch. Or perhaps this was a thirteenth-century original. The stench was overpowering – like a plastic bag of jockstraps mislaid for a week in the sauna of a brothel in Tangiers. The road began to swim before my eyes. I could already see the headlines in the local press: 'UNIVERSITY PROF SUFFOCATED BY GIANT CAMEMBERT'.

Action was called for. A road sign announced a layby. I pulled over and stopped out of smelling distance of a retired couple in a Citroën BX, who were eating fruitcake on a wooden table whose legs had been cemented to the ground to prevent tourists nicking it. I opened the door and took the Livarot for a walk, as if I was taking the dog for a pee. No one was looking, the couple were engrossed in their cake, so I gave the plastic bag a few whirls in mid-air to disperse the gas build-up. A surreptitious snifflet. In vain. The pong was as strong as ever. I was tempted to dump it in a litter bin but I couldn't bring myself to do it. A cheese is a living organism. The RSPCA would be after me ('PROF ABANDONS THREE-MONTH-OLD LIVAROT IN LITTER BIN'). The cheese, the emblem of my new-found freedom, began to weigh heavy. The colonel was getting restless.

'Stop farting around, man!'

'Yes, colonel! Of course, colonel!'

The retired couple smiled at each other knowingly, nodding in the direction of the largish gentleman in a panama talking to his cheese.

'*Ah! Ces Anglais . . .*'

I could of course shut the thing away in the boot. Unfortunately it was full of my clobber – books and clothes rather haphazardly thrown in at the last minute – and they would all be instantly impregnated by the smell. I didn't want to spend chic evenings in Paris wearing shirts that stank like a Norman's armpit. If I'd still had the old Volvo I could have concealed it way up in the back of the car, behind the grid designed to stop the labrador licking the back of your neck on tight corners. But I'd swapped the Volvo for a red Mazda. The distance between nose and boot was now insufficient. One solution remained. I'd have to put it on the roof rack. I found the bungee cords conveniently stored at the back of the boot under a box containing my rusting fresh-pasta machine. I then placed the cheese on the rack and made several loops to stop it moving around. No easy job installing a cheese on a metal structure designed for more copious luggage. At the last minute, when everything seemed in place, one of the hooks popped off its strut and slapped me on the nose. At least the olfactory orifice was momentarily numbed by the blow. I moved off, windows closed – with the sun beating down on the Livarot the smell would be intensified and could throttle me at the wheel. I drove slowly – the bulk of the cheese inevitably impairing the sleek, aerodynamic design of the car.

When the colonel, the car and myself finally made it to the motorway toll-booth, the girl behind the desk got a full whack of roof-ripened Livarot between the eyes. I tried to temper her shock with my second French joke. I smiled, as for a photograph, showing my teeth.

'*Fromage!*'

Jokes travel as badly as cheese.

2

What exactly was I doing this hot Saturday on the Rouen–Paris motorway in my red Mazda with its unpasteurized flashing light?

For a long time I had been secretly troubled by the idea that I wanted to live in France. First there was the language. I'd had a French mistress at primary school – she was married to a local businessman – and a French master at secondary. I was in love with the first and in awe of the second. When they spoke French, they were different, exciting, electric. I'd always wondered who I might be if I could speak it. Then there was the country. I suffered from a kind of nostalgia for something I'd never known. This sneaking feeling was exacerbated when the rain formed a puddle in the tarpaulin over the pond at the bottom of the garden, when moss crept like athlete's foot between the carrots, when the bread tasted of pap, and the baker's was empty at four. I occasionally dreamed of packing a suitcase and heading for Dieppe. At least I'd arrive in time to buy a loaf.

Then, one day, a letter arrived on the mat offering me a year's sabbatical leave in France.

I had submitted – not, I admit, with much conviction – a research outline to the University of Swindon. Specialist, until now, in the acquisition of English, I proposed to dedicate my time to studying how people forgot it. On the spot in France I would record ex-pats who had a tongue in each camp. Thanks to this book, entitled *Losing English*, I would change glasses and be interviewed on television by girls with long legs. The new Head of Department – Richard Badger, a curly linguistics professor with a convertible Alfa and perfect teeth – was enchanted to offer me the opportunity. It was a gentleman's agreement. His enthusiasm no more to put up with my sardonic smile the other side of his desk was only matched by my own desire no longer to tolerate his unctuous competence. If I had told him I was leaving for the wilds of Africa with a ladder to scrutinise the sphincter of the male giraffe, he would just as readily have complimented me on the extreme pertinence of my enterprise.

So now, if I wanted to, I could. *Pourquoi pas* indeed?

The ontological question unleashed a shock-wave which even rattled the gnomes in the garden. I consulted the team. Should I? Shouldn't I? Grumpy apart, they were unanimous. Go Michael. Tesco's formica breakfast area was quick to hum with my exciting news. Pamela, the waitress with a folded lace napkin in her hair, had spent last summer roasting on the beach at Royan. She immediately served me in French.

'*Veux-tu du confiture de l'orange?*'

'*Je veux bien. Merci très beaucoup.*'

'*Encore quelque café?*'

'*Non, je suis plein.*'

Another slice of toast and I'd be bilingual.

Thanks to membership of the EU everything was easy to arrange: I filled in form E-128 in case I was ill – you pay the doctor, get him to sign it, send it off to Newcastle and wait twelve years to be reimbursed; paid the 400 per cent supplement on the car insurance which protects you from the record death-toll on French roads, had a flick through the succinct twenty-five-page instruction booklet on how to obtain a *carte de séjour* and *Robert est votre oncle*.

I would have liked to slip away without any fuss but the village was determined not to let me *filer à l'anglaise*

(take French leave). We had to have a 'French party'.
'Come dressed as a frog!' stipulated the invitation delicately.
Abesbury under Lyme, the desirable village where I rented
a refurbished workman's cottage, was unaccustomed to this
kind of excitement. It regularly won prizes – for lawns, floral
displays, even for its tip: a tasteful marriage of green bins
and hornbeam. Above all it deserved an Emmy for *ennui*.
Nothing ever happened. The fire brigade were only ever
called out to rescue cats with vertigo on the oak on the
green, and the nearest we ever came to danger was the
purchase of a Sunday joint to prove that we were ready
to die of BSE for the country. There was a rumour that
the vicar was on Ecstasy but it turned out to be high blood
pressure.

For the party I bought some special-offer Boursin, a
rather hard low-fat camembert which the check-out girl
said could be crash-ripened in the greenhouse, and a pink
pâté de campagne in a tube, which I contemplated serving
on toothbrushes. Mrs Johnstone came up with a collection of
records by Yves Montand and Sacha Distel. The plumber's
brother was an Edith Piaf fanatic. He had her photograph in
his workshop in a frame made of copper piping. Everything
was in place. All I had to do was to rub the walls with garlic
and we were in business.

What was I going to wear? I briefly flirted with the idea
of going as the decapitated Louis XIVth but being headless
at the same time as I was legless would make life impossible.
Then I had a bright idea. An old double-breasted suit, a
moustache made from the remains of a cuddly animal
discarded in the back of a cupboard, *The Times*, a brolly . . .
There'd be a special prize for the first person to crack my
disguise.

The party was announced for seven. The guests began to
arrive at five to.

Anthony Brick, the interior decorator, confected a *képi*
out of a cornflakes packet and came as General de Gaulle.

Harold Holms came as a member of the French Resistance wearing the collar of his wife's trenchcoat turned up. As the mac was too small and buttoned tight he was very red in the face and looked more like Boris Yeltsin. Peter Blake wore the classic striped breton pullover complete with a string of onions – which turned out to be real, smelly and uncomfortable for his dancing partners. Maurice Hope, an insurance agent who had a topiary head of Margaret Thatcher at the entrance to his thatched cottage, had made himself a red *légion d'honneur* for his buttonhole. We spent the evening pulling on it like a door bell and going rrrrriiiinnnggggg. Brian Topps was very brown after his holiday on the Costa Brava and had found himself a rasta wig. He was supposed to be the tennis star Yannick Noah but no one had heard of Yannick Noah and everyone thought he was a mop. Robert Scott, fat and full of himself, was wearing a false nose. Everybody called him '*mon général*' and saluted, which made him angry as he believed he was the spitting image of Gérard Depardieu.

The most surprising were the ladies. Anyone driving by accident through Abesbury that Saturday evening wouldn't have believed his eyes. The main street – which stretches from the surviving sub-post office to St John's Church, passing by the seed merchants and the souvenir shop – looked like Pigalle on a hot summer night. Extraordinary creatures, encased in tight satin, their breasts welling up and out of their laced bodices like cream boiling over from a saucepan, waited on the pavements under the lampposts as their husbands parked the Rover. 'Hello darling, looking for a good time?' they called out to Bob Foster as he drove his muck-spreader back to the farm, with the result that he nearly ran over Maurice Hope's neurotic labrador.

And me? Dark suit, bowler, the moustache fashioned from the intimate parts of a cuddly toy, I hardly looked the part. The guests complained.

'Michael!'

'I mean . . . really!'

'We were all supposed to dress froggily!'

Then suddenly Judy Parker, an opulent redhead looking like Jeanne Moreau playing Dominatrix, Queen of Garlic, saw through me.

'I've got it, Michael! *Je sais!*'

'Tell us, Judy! *Il est qui?*'

'Michael is what the French think all Englishmen are – he's *le Major* Thompson!'

'. . . new style,' I hastened to add.

What a clever idea. Bravo Michael. Both Judy and her bosom were flushed with success. I chose this moment to add to her joy by awarding her the first prize: a French kiss. Brian Parker, smouldering under his beret, will be happy to see the last of me.

At midnight we all joined the gnomes in the garden to sing 'Alouette' and 'Frère Jacques'. Glasses of sparkling Bulgarian chardonnay were raised in my honour. My pockets were full of addresses in case of need – including a guaranteed supply of Marmite and Worcester Sauce in the Dordogne some 500 kilometres south of Paris. High spot of the closing ceremony – I was presented with a copy of *A Year in Provence* signed by the whole village. The book was given to me in a box which also contained a pair of Union Jack braces. The injunction to keep the flag flying greatly amused the nudge-nudge contingent. As we took leave, kissing each other at least six times on each cheek in what was supposed to be a French manner, the village resounded to cries of '*Au revoir*', '*Bonne chance*' and even a surprising '*Vive la France!*' This triggered off an immediate response from the drunk Bob Scott who sang 'God Save the Queen' in the spectral orange light of the lamppost on to which he was hanging.

Such was France as viewed from the cliffs of Abesbury under Lyme.

The next morning, as I drove out of the sleepy village, the curtains were still closed. It was a sign. England had been my pillow.

La France serait mon réveil.

3

Nigel Stokes, a gym master in the Abesbury comprehensive who had come to the party as Brigitte Bardot complete with stiff petticoat and beehive hairdo, had given me the address of a friend who could lend me a flat in Paris while I was looking for one of my own. Max, an Air France steward, who spent most of time in the ex-Eastern Bloc countries, was away at the beginning of September. His pad was in the rue de Tombouctou – Timbuctoo in French – in the 18th. The *arrondissement* system works in a snail pattern, curling out and around itself like a chocolate from the 1st – the Opéra. The 18th was out on one of the horns – paradoxically, given the address, closer to Helsinki than the Sahara. But geography has little to do with exoticism. And the address I couldn't resist.

There is a New York-style inner circular road which wends its way around Paris. It is often built on stilts which are plastered with posters of pinups on the phone advertising what the French fancifully call the *téléphone rose*. I didn't get in the right lane at the right time to exit Porte de Pantin and made a second trip around this *périphérique* which gave me a chance to examine my new territory – the industrial north, the luscious west and the commercial south, the Seine and the gares de Lyon and d'Austerlitz in the east. In the rue de Tombouctou I had to find a *truquet* – it turned out to be a *troquet*, slang for a cheap restaurant, but Nigel's handwriting suffered from several years of mishandling medicine balls – called Chez Ali where Max had deposited his keys.

After a mere forty minutes I was lucky enough to find a parking space directly in front of Chez Ali. It was a small-ish, unkempt-looking establishment with dusty windows with minaret transfers, and dark scarlet drawn curtains. A crooked sign in the right-hand window announced *Couscous à toute heure* which I didn't follow. Inside it was rather dark, and there was souk music coming from a small transistor in the back room. I seemed to have barged in on a North African whist drive. My opening – '*Excusez-moi de vous déranger. Je cherche monsieur Ali*' – caused some amusement but served to break the ice. 'Monsieur Ali,' they repeated amongst themselves gutturally.

The gentleman in question appeared from the back room, his gold tooth an oasis of light in the dim bar. Ali was young, pleasant, and plump. I ventured my opening gambit which I had had time to compose during my circular tour of the capital.

'*Bonjour, Monsieur Ali. Je suis un ami de Max . . . Excusez-moi de vous déranger mais—*'

I'd obviously spoken the magic word.

'*Un ami de Max est un ami d'Ali!*'

Ali shook me vigorously by the hand, the whist drive hummed its approval, and he led me to a table in a corner of the room on which there was a paper tablecloth, a knife and fork and a cruet.

'*Couscous!*'

I tried to explain to Ali that I had already had a *bouillabaisse dieppoise* and that the colonel was risking sunstroke outside on the roof rack. In vain.

'*Couscous royal!*'

There was no arguing. I absent-mindedly dipped a piece of bread in the red mustard in the cruet which turned out to be *harissa* – desert gunpowder used to start camels on damp mornings. Fortunately the couscous arrived and I doused the fire in the sauce. I now understood the sign in the window. '*Couscous à toute heure*' means that if you venture into

Chez Ali at any time of the night or day you are obliged to eat couscous. I made a mental note. If I come home late after dinner, I'll crawl past the windows to avoid a *merguez* nightcap.

Fifty minutes later, slightly full after my unexpected North African high tea, I found myself, keys in hand, faced with the four locks of the front door of Max's flat – two charming small rooms giving on to a narrow courtyard, a tiny kitchen and a bathroom which require delicate entry and exit procedures. If I'm ever coming out naked I must remember to do so in a state of calm. I installed the colonel on the window sill – immediately silencing a charming yellow bird in a cage opposite – and stretched out on the *canapé*. Home at last. It was then that I saw them.

The walls were draped with fishermen's nets. Inside the nets, caught like fish in the tackle, was a series of photographs arranged at jaunty angles. All the photographs were the same – portraits of legionnaires wearing their képi and very little else. Were Y-fronts the new uniform of the Foreign Legion? On a closer look I was also impressed by the fact that, unless they were cheating by means of rolled handkerchiefs or *quenelles de veau*, they filled their underpants with great enthusiasm.

The colonel, perhaps jealous of my new-found military interest, whistled at me from the window sill. I took him in, the bird started to sing again. I opened a bottle of Australian red bought on the boat, took a slice of the Mazda-matured Livarot on a chunk of baguette. Heaven. Then, feeling somewhat weary and full after the food and the journey, I slipped out of my trousers, stretched out on Max's satin sheets and dozed off.

I must have slept for some time because when the door opened it was already dusk. Max, who was not in Eastern Europe after all, had popped by with two legionnaire friends to make sure everything was OK. Small, sharp-featured, with the darting eyes of a witty ferret, Max eyed my non-regulation Fruit of the Loom boxer shorts with an air of disapproval but was at the same time most welcoming.

'*Michel!*'

I was delighted to be translated.

'The flight was cancelled. Just popped by to drop off my things.'

'Oh but Max, please, you musn't . . . I can go to a hotel. I haven't unpacked . . .'

Max would hear nothing of it.

'*Cool Michel. Cool. On va grignoter un bout ensemble.* We'll have a bite to eat and I'll kip at the barracks!'

Max was delighted with his 'kip' and repeated it several times, which explained why he didn't hear me when I told him that I had already eaten a *bouillabaisse dieppoise*, a *couscous royal* and a Livarot sandwich.

'Boys! *Au boulot!* Down to work. There's some Panzani in the cupboard!'

The two legionnaires stripped down to the waist – true, they weren't built for aprons – and set about preparing their speciality, which was *spaghetti à la vodka*. Max sat down with me on the satin sheets and gave me a brief lecture on baroque opera. *Castor et Pollux* by Rameau (1737) was doubtless his all-time favourite. Sadly he hadn't time to sing me the '*Air gai pour les athlètes*' because the spaghetti was ready. We ate *sur le pouce* – 'on the thumb' apparently either means quickly or sprawling over the bed – and because they were certain I needed a good night's kip, the Panzani division raised camp at 23.10.

The next morning, before leaving, I scribbled a note for Max thanking him for his great kindness. I also left some flowers, a truffle in a tin and a transparent plastic dome with a model of Buckingham Palace which snowed inside when you shook it. Max had been very hospitable; I felt inadequate. I knew I should have stripped to the waist and knocked up a *lapin chasseur*. But I didn't fancy ending up in the net. I left the keys with Ali, firmly refusing a *café couscous*.

Back on the *périph* – I picked up the abbreviation from Ali – I drove to the south side of Paris and found a hotel just after the exit Porte d'Orléans. My room with its delicate matching colour scheme – brown walls, brown bedspread, brown tapwater – was just what I was looking for: independence.

I decided I had to find a place of my own before the end of September when the students return and snap everything up. Where am I going to spend the year? I bought the *Indispensable de Paris* – and with the aid of the *arrondissement* maps, street names and an ever-cool, springlike mid-morning sauvignon in the Bar des Sports, set about choosing from the menu. Anything multi-syllabled, hyphenated or double-barrelled was immediately elbowed.

'*Vous habitez où?*'

'*J'habite place Richard-de-Coudenhove-Kalergi.*'

By the time I'd given my address the taxi would be in Marseilles. I quite fancied the rue Adolphe Pinard – '*pinard*' meaning 'booze' – and the passage du Désir appealed to my libidinous streak, as did the rue des Deux-Boules – although I wasn't sure I wanted to own up to living in Testicle Street, if indeed that's what it meant. Other names were less attractive. Rue Agar sounded sick. 'I feel *un peu agar ce matin*.' As did rue de la Tacherie ('he had a nasty bout of *tacherie* when he was eight'). Rue Dieu was too arrogant, rue Vassou too subservient ('He was a *vassou* chez Citroën for twenty-five years'). Impasse Rothschild was ridiculous. The most apposite was rue du Tunnel but I didn't want to be reminded of home.

I set about decoding the small ads in *Le Figaro* – which, on Tuesdays and Thursdays, is the best bet for finding a flat. The choice was vast but bewilderingly hieroglyphic. '*Un P de T, dble séj + 2 chbres, balc, ét élevé, asc, est-ouest*' read like an inscription on Ramses' tomb. Illumination was provided by a second sauvignon: a double living room (*double séjour*), two bedrooms (2 *chambres*) and a balcony (*balcon*) looking both east and west on the upper stories (*étage élevé*) served by a lift (*ascenseur*) in a smart stone (*pierre de taille*) Haussmann-style building. To keep in trim I'd better plump for *sans asc*. But I'd need stairs. Without an *esc* how would you climb the *ét*?

Next. A pad suitable for *prof lib*? I was doubtless a *prof symp*, even *sup*, but *lib*? *Prof lib* turned out to mean *profession libérale* – doctors, dentists, lawyers – salaries of that ilk. This one was also *sur verd*. Anything within spitting distance of greenery (*verdure*) was out of spitting distance of my price range. *Sur* concrete was more what I was looking for. *Vue dég* foxed me initially. *Vue dégueulasse*? Why advertise that the flat gives on to a poxy wasteland? Wrong again. '*Dég*' = *dégagée* – open (feminine agreement for *vue*). Equally upmarket were *les moulures*, which I first took to be a free portion of mussels (*marinières*?) with each flat taken. No. *Moulures* = ornamental stucco. I must be careful what I order in restaurants. As far as cooking was concerned I would clearly prefer *une cuis* to a *une k.ette* otherwise there wouldn't be enough room to sw a ct. What the hell was *un box*? A box?! At that price? Did the homeless buy *Le Figaro* in order to rent their packing case? For rent: *Hermès box vue dég s. Seine*? A box turned out to be a space in an underground car park. About the same price as the cottage in Abesbury. The Mazda would sleep in the street.

All this jargon alarmed me. What if they spoke it as well? I imagined the scene in the estate agents . . .

'*Bonj M* (Gd mo).'
'*Bonj M* (Gd mo).'
'*Je ch un app P. ch* (I'm lo. f. a cheap fl).'
'*Paris ou pr ban* (Paris or cl. sub).'
'*Rive G. si poss* (Lft b. if poss).'
'*Bien. V. vlez un caf? Un choc? Un t?*'

Undeterred, I took a series of rendez-vous; the technique was soon mastered. You turn up about ten minutes before the agreed time and find yourself outside on the pavement with about fifty other candidates who have also taken the same appointment. Everyone pretends to be doing something else – loitering with intent, learning about mushrooms and varicose veins in the window of the *pharmacie* – but you know full well that you are all there to be the first to get your hands on this potential gem, this ultimate snip amongst flats. No one queues, this is against the national adventure ethic which turns every single operation of everyday life into a competition. The human race is no metaphor in France. As soon as the doors open – the flat is in a building with a digicode which you will eventually discover is a farce, even the local dogs know it – you all rush into the doorway and up the stairs at the same time. Curiously, complaining doesn't happen *à l'anglaise*. Where in Britain one might be compelled to express polite surprise – 'Excuse me, madame, but your Yorkshire terrier has its tail up my nose' – in France you speak to yourself: '*C'est pas possible! Mais quelle bousculade! Mais qu'est-ce qu'ils ont à pousser comme ça?!*'

In truth the order of arrival is of no consequence whatsoever. Selection takes place on other criteria. All you have to do is to convince the landlord you are a rich, Catholic, right-wing non-smoker with no pets and not the slightest predilection for chaining girls to the radiator after eight o'clock at night and you're in. Before cottoning on, I managed not to be selected for: a furry box with beige carpeting on the floors and walls suitable for a retired teddy bear; a minute white flat with the kind of massive, oppressive wooden beams – *poutres apparentes* – you associate with a medieval castle, a stylish feature which doubled the rent; an *apprt mod* which smelled very strongly of dmp; and an attractive two-roomed flat above a pizzeria with oregano carpeting and mozzarella curtains. In the end I decided to change what the French call my *look* – Levi's and desert boots made in South Korea from Monoprix – for the more reassuring neo-grunge gentleman-farmer look – blue Oxford cotton button-down shirt and battered brogues. It worked. I was immediately selected (one out of thirty-three) for a flat in the 6th. And I am now the happy future tenant of a simple two-room garret in the rue de l'Abbé Grégoire just off the rue du Cherche-Midi. I've always loved the name of the street – apparently explained by the sun dial on the front of a shop showing someone looking for something too late – *midi* at *quatorze heures* as the saying goes. The flat is 7 *ét s. asc.* There is a French expression for to be very content: *être aux anges*. In this flat I am almost literally up with the angels.

Seated at my table in the Bar des Amis I read through the lease – the *bail*. This afternoon I am to sign it in the offices of the *administrateur de biens* in the rue de Rennes. Monsieur Rossi is a short, thick-set smiling man who looks like a cross between David Niven and Caruso. He always wears braces over a violet-coloured Lacoste sports shirt and smokes an eternal cigar, the sucking end of which is as damp as a labrador's nose. The decoration of his office is in tune with the paradoxical impression he gives of being a gentleman mafioso – on the left a chic black-and-white print of La Baule, bourgeois watering-place of impeccable credentials, and on the left a hand-tinted chromo of the bay of Ajaccio, France's answer to Corleone. The place is inhabited by a harem of devoted middle-aged ladies and a large number of rubber plants suffering from a lack of light and an excess of water.

The lease in its brown paper envelope is as thick as a novel, and studying it calls for yet further glasses of illuminating sauvignon. I have been allotted cellar number 17 (for my world-famous collection of bag-in-the-box Pétrus) and *boîte à lettres* number 8. I also enjoy the *jouissances des équipements privatifs*. What private equipment? I thought *jouissance* meant orgasm ... I am not permitted to dismantle the doors nor to knock holes in the walls – the Rembrandt will have to make do with sellotape – nor am

I allowed to put flowers, washing or birds on the balcony.
I am strictly forbidden to turn the flat into a nightclub, or
a Turkish bath. I cannot sub-let, use it for professional
purposes, sneeze after eleven o'clock at night or urinate in
the geraniums. In order to renounce the lease the procedure
is simple: twenty-three registered letters will do the trick. If
I do nothing to renounce it I will be 'tacitly reconducted'
and obliged to remain there for ever – a lease for life.

Rossi gives me a shark's grin as his secretary, Odile, mid-
forties, twinset, flat shoes and bun, emerges from behind a
rubber plant to bring us pen and blotting paper. Signed for
agreement.

Lu et approuvé.

4

The French share with the hedgehog the reputation of both being extremely prickly to meet and of dying in large numbers on the roads. This reputation is not wholly true. As far as hospitality is concerned, if you present yourself as someone invitable you will be invited. If, on the other hand, you turn up on the doorstep with a large rucksack, refuse the pastis because it reminds you of aniseed balls, and examine your plate as if you were looking for your false teeth in a urinal, you are unlikely to enter this category. What the French most love – that is, apart from a handful of avid readers of the *National Geographic* who would swoon with delight to find a pygmy and his mini in-laws on the doormat – is the idea that every foreigner is a potential convert to the great cause of Frenchness.

On arriving in Paris I rang Bernard Dubost, the friend of a friend in London who works in publishing. An invitation was immediately forthcoming. I am invited to dinner on Thursday at his flat just off the Bastille. I looked it up. The taking of the Bastille heralded the beginning of the Revolution. The governor's head was paraded around the streets on a pike. It is now a trendy area on the right bank.

'*Vers 20.30?*'

'Perfect.'

'Just a minute!' said Bernard just before ringing off. 'Got a pencil? I must give you the digicode.'

'The . . . ?'

And he gives it to me in gunfire French. '*Deuxcent-quaranteseptAsoixantedeux.*'

And adds: '*EscalierDsurcourquatrièmegauche.*'

Click. Gulp.

Thursday evening at 19.30 I made my entrance into the local florist's, Monceau Fleurs on the boulevard Raspail. The place was rather overpowering. You can buy anything from a bunch of violets to a real palm tree with a plastic monkey. I was looking for something suitable for Bernard, who is in his forties, balding and divorced. The assistant followed my gaze and mistook confusion for choice. He took a bunch from a display bucket and presented it as if he wanted to propose to me.

'*Les renonculacées* never fail to please.'

French *fleuristes* are red-hot at this game. They spend hours in the loo learning the Vilmorin seed catalogue off by heart, and then beat you into abject submission by their superior knowledge. He put the boot in in Latin, adding something that went like '*Encolitus hibernatus*'.

I'm up against a *swotassus latrinus*. But I'm not going to lose face. I snatched a prepacked bunch in a blue bucket at my feet.

'These! Ah. Now! These! These are what I was looking for.'

I gave him the bouquet. It was a long stemmy bunch ending with rather attractive little bells. I've always had a penchant for bells and was not displeased with my choice.

'*C'est pour offrir?*'

Are they a present? This question, inevitably asked by French florists, has never ceased to bemuse me. I would like to have replied, 'No, actually they're not a present. I'm going to conceal a four-kilo lead weight in them and when my ex-wife answers the door I'm going to say, "Darling, this is for you" and . . . THUMP!' What I believe the Kray brothers referred to as the floral bonjour.

I would like to tell Jean-Claude how much easier things

are in England. In England it's a piece of cake. You go into the florist's and say: 'I'll have the blue ones.' At which the young man with two rings in his eyebrows rolls the bunch up nice and tight in brown paper with as much ease as if he was rolling a joint – indeed leaving you the option, when you get home, of smoking the bunch if you've gone off the colour – and you're through. None of the *hibernatus* psychodrama.

When I took the métro at Saint-Placide I realised I had made an error of chronology. I should have (a) taken the métro; (b) bought the flowers. It was extremely difficult to protect my rather spindly spray in a carriage tightly packed with harrassed shop assistants, young men in bomber jackets bearing the name of American basketball teams and, between Saint-Sulpice and Saint-Michel, two Romanians playing a fifty-two-second version of the highlights from *Cavalliera Rusticana*. I was obliged to move my bunch about in mid-air looking like an RAF officer signalling in a Harrier jet with a bunch of indigo tinker bells. I came out of the wrong exit at the Bastille and found myself admiring the rather unlikely vista of a lot of smart boats and barges tied up along a quay. This urban maritime scene was not without its charms but a stiff sea breeze whipped off the Seine and the transparent cellophane over my bunch cracked like a spinnaker under strain. I stuffed the flowers upside-down inside my jacket to protect them. The tinkerbells now poked out of the bottom. I crossed the crowded place de la Bastille looking like Bacchus in a Marks & Sparks tweed jacket with a floral codpiece.

I arrived at the address. Disaster. I'd forgotten the envelope with the digital code and I didn't have a mobile. What the hell was the number? 2030? Didn't work. Not surprising. That was time I was invited for. And it was already 20.45. The café on the corner was about to close, the brown formica chairs were upturned on the tables and the patron in his shirt sleeves was rummaging in his sink behind the bar. He didn't look up, doubtless wary of a last-minute piss artist who'd stop him going home.

'*Excusez-moi, monsieur*. I've stupidly mislaid the digicode for number 14.'

Ungraciously, he lifted his head, removed his hands from the sink and wiped them on his stained fawn terylene trousers.

'*Et alors?*'

Mental note. Ring the Michelin guide tomorrow morning. Welcome: 2 out of 10.

'I'm in a bit of a fix. I'm invited to dinner at number 14 and I can't get in.'

He was unimpressed by my charmingly British incompetence.

'Even if I had the number, I wouldn't give it to you.'

I waved my tinkerbells at him and attempted a rather complicated sentence involving a subordinate clause and a subjunctive which in English went something like this: 'Surely, even if you had suspected me, these flowers should be a convincing guarantee of my credentials?'

No reply. Not surprising, as the syntactical construction took me some five minutes. New tack.

'I think I'll have a small Beaujolais.'

He fished a sticky glass out of the mirey aquarium in which it had been macerating since early that morning, gave it a peremptory wipe with a tea towel last seen in Balzac's *La Comédie humaine* and slopped a warm Beaujolais on the counter. Throwing my 17 francs into a drawer which served as a till, he looked at me with a beady eye.

'And what, monsieur, what stops a burglar from buying a bunch of flowers? *Hein?*'

I was taken aback by his argument. Sensing my hesitation he leapt into the breach and leaned on the bar, suddenly interested in my predicament now he was certain he could avoid helping me.

'All these men walking around the streets with bunches

of flowers? Is it normal? Where they going? What they up to? Who says they're not burglars taking you for a ride? *Hein?*'

I had never thought of it like that. He stabbed the zinc with a stubby finger, pursuing his remorseless logic.

'If there are so many flower shops in the rich *quartiers*, there must be a reason, *non?*'

His argument was too much for me and I gave up. By the time I was back in front of number 14 it was already nine o'clock. Both bouquet and guest were rapidly beginning to wilt. I crossed the road and tried shouting from the other side: '*Monsieur Dubost! Monsieur Dubost!*'

A jaded pigeon toying with a slice of damp garlic sausage looked down disparagingly from his window sill. He knew as well as me that Dubost lived *sur cour*. No reaction from one or two passers-by who took me for a nutter. If there was no joy in the next five minutes I'm going to take the métro home, ring to apologise and eat the bells for supper.

At that precise moment a group of four people arrived in front of number 14 and tapped authoritatively on the digicode. My last chance! I ran straight across the road, narrowly missing a bus coming in the opposite direction, and arrived just in time to wedge my foot in the closing door. The group turned as a man to confront the intruder. Puffed and spluttering I told my story which they either didn't believe or understand. They reluctantly allowed me to enter.

We found ourselves in a maze of corridors and stairways. I couldn't for the life of me remember what Bernard had told me on the phone . . . *escalier* . . . something *porte* . . . God knows what. So as not to give the impression that I was a burglar with a bunch I followed them. They held the door for me, I held the door for them. Everyone very proper in the semi-darkness.

'*Merci, monsieur.*'

'*Je vous en prie, monsieur.*'

We arrived at the lift, pressed the button and waited in silence. When it finally arrived it was extremely cramped and had a metallic door which closed like a sharp concertina, nearly making a ham sandwich of my left buttock.

'Which floor, *monsieur*?'

I couldn't press the button myself, hampered by the flowers and lack of space. Fortunately I could remember. Fourth.

'*Quatrième, s'il vous plaît, monsieur.*'

All this formal 'monsieur' business was slightly incongruous as I had my nose in between his shoulder blades and my flowers over my head. Fourth floor. Everyone got out. I was about to pretend to remember whether it was right or left when the door on the landing opened and, surprise surprise, Bernard Dubost in person greeted us.

'So you all came up together! Did you introduce yourselves?'

Once inside the flat the group from the lift immediately defrosted. Cold outside, warm in. We smiled at each other and introduced ourselves – an attractive blonde in a Chanel suit, a striking brunette in trousers, a fat fast-speaking man in tweed hiding behind a Gitanes smokescreen, a very thin-looking intellectual in a black suit and matching T-shirt and what appeared to be a banker who has just emerged from a *pince-fesses* – a 'bottom pincher' – the name for a cocktail party. When Bernard told them I was English they all smiled and exclaimed, '*Ah! Ça s'explique!*'

What exactly it explained I didn't attempt to fathom. Bernard politely enquired if the flowers were for him – flustered, I was still holding on to the bunch – and was very touched for he too had a weakness for little bells. Another couple arrived. The evening could get under way.

The host served the apéritif: three whiskies, three glasses of red wine, a fruit juice and a Pernod. A Pernod! Everyone seemed to find the Pernod a hoot.

'You want to play *pétanque*, Jean-Damien?'

And the badinage began. Fasten your seatbelts.

First subject of conversation: a sociological classification of apéritifs. Is Banyuls bourgeois and Chivas chic? Pastis, I learned, is decidedly *plouc* which I thought sounded very pleasant, like the noise made by two ice cubes rubbing shoulders, but no, Bernard tells me *plouc* means unsophisticated. I retired into my inner sanctum to compose an elegant sentence which involved a reflection upon my aunt and the gin bottle but when I emerged, too late, the conversation had already moved on. They were debating the latest Eric Rohmer movie. Soap, *tarte* (tart?) or Marivaux? *Tarte* and *plouc* are apparently close cousins. I popped back to the sanctum to cobble together a recollection of *Ma Nuit chez Maud* but when I hit the surface again they were on to the strained relations between president and prime minister and some acid *petite phrase* pronounced on the steps of the Elysée. I'll never catch up. I'm an elephant running after a will o' the wisp.

The food was ready. Ready was perhaps not quite the word. No one seemed to dare tell Bernard he had forgotten to put the beef in the oven. I've heard of *saignant* but this was ridiculous. Someone who was either courteous or colour-blind referred to the meat as *bleu,* which seemed to meet general approval. I made a mental note. If I invite people to dinner, no need to cook the food. Just tell them the greens are blue and everyone's happy.

Sensing my confusion the sparkling brunette came to my assistance. *Bleu*, she began to explain, is an adjective which dates from the time that the cossacks used to slip their steak between their bum and the saddle in order to cook it. The dye from their trousers subjected the steak to inordinate friction . . . But she never finished the sentence. Eating didn't stop them talking and the wine – a light and attractively chewy Côtes-du-Rhône – accelerated the action. They were on to public-service broadcasting. The debate was led by a short-sighted TV journalist who talked like a machine gun with diarrhoea. All I could catch were the first and last words of each sentence. Between these two banks, like Ariane on a tightrope, I attempted to walk my thread. In the end I gave up, served myself another glass of wine and went on strike. I jotted down on a napkin the subjects broached during the raw meat course: giving up cigarettes; big tits; minimalism; football and national identity; a Mexican revolutionary called the subcomandante Marcos; the discovery of an excellent cheap champagne; not paying parking fines; big tits.

Then. The high spot of the evening. The guided tour.

Bernard stood and, with a twinkle in his eye . . .

'I think that perhaps now we should take a little walk in the garden . . .'

A garden on the fourth-floor escalier D next door to the Bastille?! When I asked the question the other guests gave me a nudge and put their fingers to their lips . . . *Chut!* Mum's the word. The mystery deepened. Glasses in hand we left the table and crossed the salon into Bernard's bedroom. There, with due solemnity, he opened the heavy cherrywood door of an old country-style wardrobe, moved aside the curtain formed by several pairs of rather boring-looking trousers and, like a magician, unveiled his *arboretum*: six rather sickly-looking cannabis plants warming themselves like baby chickens under the heat bulb. Bernard was over the moon. It was his chamber version of the Medellín cartel. We were all suitably impressed by his skill and his daring, standing there breathing in the distant smell of *le shit* – grass – mixed with that, rather more pungent, of his dry-cleaned trousers, for all the world like a group of junkies in Monet's garden at Giverny.

'It's a very delicate business,' the gardener explained. Last week the bulb he bought was too powerful and it discoloured his brogues. The cultivation of the illicit is a path of thorns.

Back in the salon, almost flat out in the low slung leather

dumpling-style armchairs, they all agreed: the major problem facing Western society today is *les cons* (Collins Robert: damn fools, bloody [Brit] idiots, cretins). Apparently they are easily recognisable (they have *têtes de con*), move around in groups (*des bandes de cons*) and have a lot of children (*des petits connards*). But even in agreement the guests give the impression that they are in the midst of a violent argument. They throw their arms up in the air, shout, gesticulate. A sentence flies up into the stratosphere only to be brought down by the surface-to-air missiles fired by the launchers hidden deep in the dumplings. They go red in the face, they are apoplectic. Even the dog – a hitherto rather lethargic labrador – joins in. They stand, harangue the crowd, sit. Decapitation will doubtless ensue. The spirit of the Bastille lives on.

And then, just as suddenly as it had started, the debate came to an end. As if Cupid had descended from the flies at the end of the operetta they all decided that enough was enough, they all had to work tomorrow morning and it was time to go home. The women kissed the women, the men kissed the men and we all agreed that we were off to join subcomandante Marcos in the heart of the Mexican jungle. They're still in full form; I'm exhausted.

'That's the problem with the *gauche caviar*,' Bernard Dubost told me afterwards. 'It's much better to talk than to listen.'

Gauche caviar? A clumsy sturgeon? No. The term used for smart lefties, for the *rive gauche* Armani army. Outside, in the blurred euphoria of *une soirée arrosée* – literally, 'a watered evening', although water has little to do with the liquid consumed – on that very pavement which had threatened to be the scene of my defeat, they performed an essential French ritual. Just before going their different ways Parisians exchange visiting cards and make invitations – or rather, express the desire to make invitations – they know they will never keep.

'*Il faut qu'on se revoie.*'

'*Il faut qu'on se téléphone*' (gesture: thumb and little finger held to ear and mouth).

'*Il faut qu'on déjeune ensemble*' (gesture: the two hands about to use a knife and fork).

This is both normal and understandable. During the dinner, given the deeply personal and emotional nature of the discussion, you reveal your intimate secrets, fears and desires to a group of people that you just haven't the time to see again. How could you? Life is too short and you've already got too many friends. And so the visiting card becomes the symbol of a virtual friendship, of a contact you would, in another life, have loved to have had. Later I contemplated the first evening's haul: Elizabeth Terrier, accountant; Caroline Ponge, stylist; Ivan Terrier, journalist on F2; Jean-Damien Prince, publisher; Bastien Lescure, advertising executive. Nothing, I noted, from the sparkling brunette.

These cards can come in useful. I recently presented as my own the visiting card of an extremely tedious saxophone professor from Lille to a woman who had bored the knickers off me all evening vaunting the merits of the defoliant Round-up. I trust they'll ring each other and make lunch.

5

On Thursday I finally took leave of my brown hotel to
move into my new flat. My heterogeneous bric-à-brac in
no way called for the grey blankets and the hydraulic lifts of
the removal pros and I decided to effect the operation myself
in the red Mazda. The plan of campaign had been carefully
worked out in advance. Leaving the rue Saint Placide on
my left, passing the one-way rue de l'Abbé Grégoire and
the rue de Bérite I would turn left up the rue Jean Ferrandi,
left into the rue de Vaugirard, Paris's longest street, and left
again into the rue de l'Abbé Grégoire – this time in the right
direction.

So far so good. All was going to plan.

But on my arrival in front of the apartment block there
was nowhere to park. Not surprising. It was a Thursday
morning in the centre of Paris. I was in no hurry – the
whole day had been set aside for the move – and so I
drove around the block again taking my time: left into
Cherche-Midi admiring the '30s antiques in the shop with
its blue front, left up Jean Ferrandi past the very attractive
artists' studios covered in wisteria, left into the busy rue de
Vaugirard and back again into L'Abbé Grégoire, where no
one has moved.

Determined to be patient to the point of zen, I was just
about to do my third tour when I glimpsed the butcher in
his white apron eyeing me from the doorstep of his shop.
So as not to lose face – I am new to the *quartier* and
don't want to give the impression that I am in any way

ill-equipped to contend with the demands of the city – I decided to do what I've seen all Parisians doing. I stopped the car, double-parked and opened the boot.

Immediately a pink Fiat Punto drew up about a yard from my rear bumper. The driver, a young man with a pronounced five o'clock shadow, rap thumping out of the car, didn't move but tapped the wheel with one finger in rhythm to the music and looked in my direction with an aggressive vacuity. My glands, which until that moment had adapted themselves extremely well to the Continent, suddenly started to irrigate my system with Anglo-Saxon enzymes. In a word I felt embarrassed. I didn't want to put people out.

English embarrassment is ontological. We constantly reduce ourselves to the state of being unnecessary fleas on the face of the universe. I've often told my French friends, how can you recognise an Englishman abroad in the dark? Easy. Go into any big Parisian cinema after the start of the film. Choose a seat in the middle of the row. Enter the row taking care to tread on everyone's foot. The first person you tread on who apologises will be English. It's infallible.

Embarrassment is far more low-profile in France. The word exists but is more common in its absent form – *sans gêne* – than as any positive manifestation. There is an important No Parking sign, *Stationnement gênant*, which in effect means that if you leave your car unattended for more than an hour it will be towed away to the compound called the *pré-fourrière*. *Gênant* in this sense obviously means – given the number of Parisians who run the deadly risk – *gênant* for others and not for yourself. Therein lies the difference. In fact, I don't think I have ever seen a Frenchman blush.

So I pretended to be French. I brazenly opened the boot and nonchalantly took out a suitcase and a green plant which I carefully placed on the pavement in front of the main door – all this under the sardonic eye of the man sitting in the pink ghetto-blaster. I then casually put my hand in my inside pocket to find the digicode written on the back of an envelope to get into the apartment block. Nothing. Trousers. Nothing. Back pocket – *la poche révolver*. Nothing. I must have left it in the car. Arrogance gave way to embarrassment, embarrassment to panic.

Tant pis.

Leaving my belongings on the pavement – the butcher will keep an eye on them – I went back to the car. Vaugirard, Abbé-Grégoire, Cherche-Midi – for someone who had spent many years driving up Abesbury High Street from the sub-post office to the seed shop – was no unpleasant prospect. I started off on my third tour of the block. The butcher did, however, look relieved to see me back. The green plant was in danger of succumbing to sunstroke.

Once again I parked *en double file*, opened the boot and once again it happened. Before I could get down to work another car, this time a grey Renault Mégane, stopped even closer than the Punto behind my rear bumper. The driver had the congested complexion of a man who had had a bad morning unsuccessfully mending incomprehensible Japanese photocopiers in stressed offices.

'*Bordel!*'

A popular, vulgar exclamation indicating exasperation: 'Brothel!' A more explicit variation being '*Putain!*' But this was no time for lexical niceties.

I chose to ignore this expression of a metaphysical anguish that had more to do with life and photocopiers than with me and my move and extracted from the boot my kitchen basket with the mixer, the garlic press, Mrs Beeton, an odd selection of *saucissons* and bananas.

'*Et maintenant le voilà qui nous joue le retour des Bronzés! C'était bien les vacances? Et merde!*'

I didn't catch all of this. I identified a reference to the

Bronzés films – a French 'Carry On' series from the '80s which I had once seen when I broke down in Rouen – and equally one to the fact that I must be returning from holiday, which was of course not the case. The photocopier lit a Camel and inhaled so deeply that the smoke came out of his exhaust. I decided to do my bit for Anglo-French relations. I jumped back into the Mazda and set off again.

Once again double-parked after a record-breaking lap of the block, what had to happen, happened. I switched on the warning lights, jumped out, opened the boot, took a plastic bag, one handle of which immediately snapped, spilling its contents on to the floor of the boot, and a third car drew up behind me.

Et merde.

Only this time there was a difference. The car, I sensed, although I didn't dare look round, had pulled up at a respectful distance from the Mazda and – a sign of heaven-sent patience? – had switched off its engine. I turned slowly. I was not mistaken. The vehicle, an ageing, sedate Peugeot, had the crest of the Rotary Club or some other respectable institution on the windscreen. I was in luck. These people were classy. They were old-style conservatives. This was '*la vieille France*'. There'd be no rap or hassle to oblige me to do a fifth lap.

I re-opened the boot and extracted a pink art-déco toaster and a Tesco cardboard wine basket containing four assorted bottles of wine, a carton of milk and my aluminium olive oil spray that I can't do without but never use. And I stopped. This was appalling. Now I could, I didn't want to. To move in public is to reveal your innermost secrets. I've often looked with commiseration at battered sofas as they wait at the bottom of the removal men's lift, abandoned on the drab pavement to the ridicule of the public gaze, stripped of the cosy context in which they once looked loved and respectable.

Now I was subjected to the same horror. Emptying your

boot is like undressing on the beach. The intimacy was too much for me. So I did what you must never do in France. I acted out my embarrassment. I made fun of myself by going over the top. As I passed in front of the Peugeot with my wicker laundry basket, I pretended to be a sherpa on the slopes of Everest; as I carried a precarious load of saucepans into which I had stuffed my shoes, I did my famous Nubian slave act. The respectable middle-aged Rotary couple in the Peugeot didn't bat an eyelid. Not a smile, not a sympathetic remark. No 'Jolly hot' or 'Looks heavy!' to keep you going. Nothing. They just looked at me as if I had lost my marbles. They were joined by a pretty African traffic warden who obviously shared their concern. I was in danger of getting a ticket for over-acting. What was clear was that they would never have any trouble double-parking. To every country its immunity. Indians are immune to poverty, Eskimos to cold, the Japanese to work, the English to hypocrisy and the French to other people.

When I had finally carted all my junk up the six flights, it was a great feeling to be installed in my own flat giving on to the sun-reflecting roofs and domes of Paris. I dumped all the gear in the bedroom, leaving the *living* – the main room – empty. To hell with it. Tonight I'll sleep on the floor and buy bed and cooker tomorrow. I went back downstairs to get crisps, tomatoes, camembert, a bottle of Cotes-du-Rhône and, as I'd just moved in, some *jambon sous blister* which is not chafed skin from an athlete's ankle but vacuum-packed ham. I sat on the floorboards and ate and drank too fast.

Night fell. I listened to Alain Souchon singing 'Foule sentimentale' from the second floor:

> *Foule sentimentale*
> *Avec soif d'idéal*
> *Attirée par les étoiles, les voiles*
> *Que des choses pas commerciales ...*

I watched the crime movie on TF1 on the television opposite but gave up after the second murder. The floor was hard and I opened another bottle to soften the boards.

Aux anges.

6

I'm very attracted to the café downstairs. Le Balto has a metal topped bar – *un zinc* – and a three-tiered glass cake-stand which always includes a *pavé au chocolat* and a *gâteau à la rhubarbe* plus the *tarte* of the day. On the back wall there's a mural of skiffs tied to a wooden pier outside a 1930s-style riverside restaurant-cum-dance hall – *une guingette*. The *patron* of the Balto is tall and stooped, looks like a balding, sedate version of John Cleese, and wears the same clothes everyday – a V-necked dark blue short-sleeved pullover, checked shirt, black trousers. His real name is André but, because of his height, the whole *quartier* calls him Dédé *l'asperge*. Madame Asparagus is the vivacious, encyclopaedic blonde Gilberte. If you're ever shut out, Gilberte, unlike her gruff colleague at the Bastille, can recite all the digicodes of the adjoining *immeubles* off by heart. I never had my pub in England. I was delighted to have *mon bistro* in Paris.

Most evenings round about a quarter to eight a group of local *commerçants* – butcher, fishmonger, wine merchant – meet at the bar for an apéritif. I envied their particularly French kind of *camaraderie*. They'd kiss each other several times, tweak cheeks, pummel shoulders, and thump backs as if they were trying to dislodge a trout not a fishbone. I'd love to be bruised by *mes copains*. Shaving in the morning, I'd run through their routines.

'*Salut Michael, ça gaze?*' ('Things great?')

'*Ca boume mon vieux, ça boume.*' ('Things are fine!')

But I soon found this solitary *badinage* a bit pathetic.

I knew them all by sight. There was Monsieur Goujon, the butcher, as squat and solid as a nightclub bouncer; Francis, who ran the local Nicolas wine shop, very slight and pale for someone who worked in *gros rouge* and who was taking a body-building course to survive the rigours of delivering cases of Perrier to the seventh floor *sans asc*; Jean-Claude, the red-faced, chain-smoking photocopier salesman with the Mégane; Didier, the classy fishmonger, crewcut, smart gold-rimmed glasses and blue wellies; and, on the touchline, the other side of the bar, as wise and sardonic as a tall owl, wiping endless wine glasses with a red and white checked dishcloth, Dédé l'Asperge in person, referee and arbiter of the meetings of the *Club des cinq* – The Famous Five.

On my first visits they didn't recognise or acknowledge me. At the end of the second week Monsieur Goujon greeted me with a welcome *bonsoir monsieur* and, once he had set the ball rolling, the others followed suit. By the end of the month the formal *monsieur* had disappeared and the *bonsoir* was accompanied by a smile and an almost familiar *ça va?*

I knew their stories. Their conversations took place just along the bar from me and, paradoxically, when they lowered their voices to a dramatic whisper to emphasise the intimacy of what they were about to reveal, their diction was all the clearer. Lucien Goujon, thanks to his talent, his meat and the *quartier*, had become the butcher of the upper crust – the *gratin*. He was like an analyst who had swapped the sofa for the chopping block. He was party to the carnal desires of the great of this world. Hunched over the *billot*, a little white bob cap on his head, he would explain that he was working on a shoulder for 'Lionel' (Jospin) or on some tripe for 'Jacques' (Chirac). Last week he was rolling a rabbit for 'Françoise' (Sagan). His standing caused him problems. His clients, instead of contemplating from afar, like Greeks at the altar, the cuts intended for the gods, tried to inveigle him into parting with the star's order.

'*Le rôti de Jack [Lang] t'es sûr que tu ne veux pas me . . .*'

But Lucien Goujon assured us. There was no preferential treatment. Dustman or prince, a chop is a chop. *Une côtelette est une côtelette.* The *Club des cinq* drank to this moving declaration of democratic butchery.

Last night my ear, planted like a KGB mike in a bunch of gladioli, caught the gist of Didier's anguish. He was doubtless over-sensitive to the desiderata of his sassy clientèle. Madame Soulat had a delicate constitution? He de-boned the salmon with a pair of tweezers. Madame Jouvet would only eat French fish? He recited the pedigree of her *pageot* off by heart. Over the last few months everyone had been asking for everything filleted – from turbot to sardines. Now to fillet a fish you need time. To cut down the waiting he took on a couple of filleters. Result? The price of the fish went up to pay for the bigger payroll. Result? The queue diminished. Result? The filleters had nothing to do and were laid off. Result? The price of fish went down and the queue got bigger. A nightmare. In the evening chez Dédé l'Asperge, Didier gave vent to his spleen. The *zinc* was his confessional.

'*Allons!*' said Jean-Claude. 'You're having us on. All these problems . . . It's a load of cod.'

And they fell about laughing, thumping, pummelling and tweaking, like a bunch of Walt Disney beavers celebrating the completion of a dam. At that precise moment a glass of Sauvignon arrived on the *zinc* in front of me.

'*Pour moi, Monsieur Dédé?!*'

I had nothing against another sauvignon but I hadn't ordered it. Dédé smiled: 'It's on the gentlemen.'

And l'Asperge nodded in the direction of the *Club des cinq*. They'd stopped their thumping and were looking at me with a smile. I raised my glass in their direction and they gestured for me to join them. This was a moment of great solemnity. I was in the process of being accepted. They all spoke at the same time.

'Don't go thinking the French are inhospitable . . . *Surtout pas!*'

'We have a bad reputation. *Ah ça oui . . .*'

'It's the fault of the press.'

'*Mais la presse se trompe comme toujours.* We like the English!'

'Especially the girls . . . *A nous les petites anglaises!*'

The feminine noun was followed by general sighing, winking and swooning, although they'd probably never met any *anglaises*, which might account for their enthusiasm.

'It is a beautiful country, England. *Très joli . . .*'

'Apart from the fog . . .'

'*Ah, le brouillard!*'

And they all acted blind and drove around as if the café had been plunged into a peasouper on the M4. Goujon suddenly swerved violently to the left.

'*A gauche tous!*'

They were on the wrong side of the road! Serious collisions in the dense fog of the Balto were only avoided thanks to their amazing reflexes sharpened by at least four pastis. All in all they were chuffed to have an English drinking companion. They presumed that I'd fled the mad cows and the appalling food.

'*Ah, la bouffe anglaise . . .*'

They went into instant mourning, contemplating the horrendous world I'd left behind, where overcooked meat was served with jam. The only advantage of the fog was that it hid what was on your plate. *Pauvre rosbif!* Jean-Claude, who once spent an appalling five days at an international photocopying congress in Bournemouth, recalled in horror, 'I lost five kilos . . . *Cinq kilos!*'

Goujon commiserated. Had he known he could have faxed him a *saucisson*. And they started the routine again. Laugh, pummel, and tweak. No one has bruised me yet but I'm getting warmer. Suddenly Dédé's new SFR portable rang. It was his colleague from the Bar des Amis opposite. He wanted to know who I was.

'*C'est mon prof d'anglais. Tu ne le savais pas?* I am learning English!'

How do you say *prof d'anglais* in English?

'It izz maï ingleesshhhhh . . .'

'*Messieurs. S'il vous plaît! Ici on parle français!*'

Only French should be spoken! Jean-Claude was the only member of the club not to be over-tickled at my presence. He stood and announced to the assembled company that he was going to turn on the lawn sprinkler – *mettre le tourniquet en marche* – I jotted down the expression on the back of a métro ticket. As he left for the gents, he heaved up his trousers to just below his enormous gut, under which his belt ran like a ring road around a major conurbation. Dédé was lovingly critical: '*Jean-Claude . . . Faut faire gaffe . . .* Keep an eye on yourself . . . You should try a Montignac.'

What the hell was a Montignac? From the unappreciative noises made by the Famous Five it couldn't be anything pleasant. I did some research. Montignac is the inventor of a famous diet. Jean-Claude seemed disinclined to follow their advice. Maybe we should send him back to Bournemouth.

As dusk drew in – *vers l'angélus*, as I put it in my rather literary French, thinking of Millet, but no one at the bar gave a fart – and as the evening sun began to dapple the river and the skiffs on the wall, Dédé started stacking the chairs on the tables. The café was now empty but for the regulars. The metal shutter was already half pulled down. To leave you had to duck under it like a limbo dancer. This was a time for confidences. The club looked at each other and nodded in agreement. I had passed the test. They had an invitation for me. Once a month on a Monday – when Francis and Didier are closed – they all meet up in the backroom of the Nicolas wine store for a special lunch. And at these lunches they only eat . . . and they winked at me, five heavy left eyelids batting in the half-dark – 'forbidden food'. Absolutely 100 per cent '*in-ter-dit*'. Would I care to join them?

I accepted with pride tinged with a certain apprehension. Why forbidden?

7

I got up early to do relaxation exercises. I stretched out on the floor on my back, a book under my head. I breathed slowly and sideways like an actor preparing for a marathon performance. I was Hamlet, emptying myself of myself. I drained the tension from my body. I could feel the muscles giving way, the resistance melting. I then took a substantial athlete's breakfast: nuts, cheese, ham.

Yesterday I had bought emergency rations: chocolate, dried fruit, and Mars bars. I made a thermos of sweet tea. Everything was ready. Over the last week I had taken care to finalise the plans, to double-check routes and to calculate trajectories. Today was D-day.

Or rather . . . E-day?

I went down to the car. Lucien Goujon, on the step of his butcher's shop, wished me *bonjour. Bon courage* would be more appropriate. After a corrida in Arles you can eat the bull. This evening I could end up on a hook in his shop.

I was going to attempt the ascent by the southern route. This was not perhaps the easiest of approaches but it was the most logical. The assault was to begin at 10.46 when all should be relatively calm. The decks of the car had been cleared for action. Nothing extraneous, just the provisions on the back seat and the tactical plan sellotaped to the dashboard. All furry bears with eyes that light up when you brake, all stickers saying you'd been to Skye had been removed. The car was, like me, lean, ready.

On the left bank I felt relatively relaxed. The tension

began to mount as I reached the Pont de l'Alma. I wiped my perspiring hands on the specially prepared Kleenex. Snatch, wipe, discard. All in one motion. Clean, efficient, zen. I drove up the Avenue Marceau. Around me were cars driven by those who had done it before and lived. They were blithe. It had become part of their daily routine. But did they remember the first time?

The target was approaching. I couldn't yet see it but I could sense it. My mouth began to go curiously dry. My hands trembled. And suddenly there it was. Looming menacingly before me, huge, mythical, forbidding, the Everest of my nightmares, the Cape Horn of the motorist . . .

The Place de l'Etoile.

In the course of my life I have accepted many challenges. Never one as daunting. I looked to the left of me. A mother with her baby in a bucket seat. They had unconsciously accustomed themselves to danger. I, the novice, was the only one to know what truly was at stake. '*Nous dansons sur un volcan*,' said Jean Renoir of his film *La Règle du jeu* in 1939. He was right – we were all still blithely dancing on the rim of a volcano.

Deep breath. The light turns green, the traffic advances. This is the moment. I am Hemingway at the gates. Heart beating fast, I enter the arena.

I feel immediately like a spermatozoon looking for the right route. Can there be a way through the maelstrom? I shun introspection. No time for thought. Action is the order of the day. I attempt to maintain my course. Angle of entry: 30 degrees. Difficult. The Mazda has little choice. It is part of a gallant phalanx of cars entering from the Avenue Marceau.

There is a cornerstone of French civilisation called *la priorité à droite*. No Englishman seeking to follow in my footsteps should forget it. In a built-up area, car A must give way to car B coming fast and without looking out of a side street, intent on proving it is allowed to do so because of the existence of the law which car A, into whom car B will inevitably smash, is trying to forget. This is one part of the highway code that the French choose to respect. It is a *cause célèbre*. Some 1,830 drivers a year die in their defence of the *priorité à droite*.

Attention! She nearly hit me! I look around. On my left, a pensioner, his face reddened by the effort, on my right a lorry driven by a mason, his face white from the plaster. The pensioner doubtless left his flat in 1972 in order to buy a baguette and has been here ever since. His wife has died, his son has had triplets. He is oblivious to all this. And still he turns, baguetteless and desperate, looking for the exit. The mason was told to deliver his cement for the original construction of the Arc de Triomphe. He has never made it to the centre. A film should be made on these people, wandering, like lost souls in the outer circles of Dante's Hell. The rest of the world fades into insignificance. Moving forward is all that is of interest. Grab the next yard. Take what there is to be taken. *No pasaran!*

My stomach feels strangely empty. A mixture of hunger and fear. I reach over for a dried banana in my emergency provisions on the back seat without ever taking my eyes off what is in front of me. I stuff the dried banana into my mouth, ravenous. Odd texture. *Merde!* I've eaten a Kleenex. *Tant pis.* It will mop up the acidity.

At the best of times the Place de l'Etoile is like a vast jigsaw puzzle made up of odd pieces which don't belong together. A bit of a glacier shoved into a pot of geraniums. But occasionally heaven makes sense out of serendipity and the impossible puzzle clicks into place. What must be very beautiful from the top of the Arc de Triomphe spells traffic doom below. Nothing moves. Nothing can move. You could stay there immobile for ever. The only way out is through the window of the car. Walk across the roofs of the gridlocked puzzle and out to freedom. I'd make a fortune selling my sandwiches to less prudent motorists.

'Pitié! Le sandwich rillettes. 2000 balles!'

Then, as if by miracle, a Peugeot 205 wriggles, slaloms and loosens the lock. The whole puzzle jolts into movement, bumping, pushing, heaving, manoeuvring, cheating. We're on the move again! I've been on the Place de l'Etoile for some thirty minutes, I've made about fifty yards and I'm having the time of my life. I'm not the only one. I keep meeting the same cars. People don't come here to go anywhere. They come here for the adrenalin.

If you want to go fast, get to the centre and go round tight. OK, you get giddy, but the sense of achievement is equally heady. Like a bomber pilot you chalk up each lap on the side of the car. At the same time take the opportunity to visit the tomb of the unknown driver in the middle of the Arc de Triomphe. A Japanese family impressed by my performance turns and starts taking photographs of the Mazda.

If entering was difficult, exiting is even worse. In the eye of the storm you are protected from the turbulence of the outer circles, but when you try to move outwards the surface tension pushes you back in again. Finally I managed to follow a police car which is pushing its way through, light flashing, siren wailing, boring its way through the compact mass of cars. The next time I'll do the same. With a Livarot in the place of the flashing light.

Like a gymnast falling on his feet after a triple somersault, I managed to exit Avenue Marceau – the road by which I came in. I parked the car in a *contre-allée* – the side road running parallel to the main road – and went into a bar to down a pick-me-up. Since mid-morning all I'd eaten was three dried bananas, eight dates, twenty-three apricots and a Kleenex. I had a hard-boiled egg and a cognac, an odd mix but it was what I fancied. My legs were shaking with the release of nervous tension. *Je l'ai fait!* I'd done it. One day, in the distant future, on a Sunday evening, with my grandchildren perched on my knees around the fire, as the embers glow in the horse brass, I'll tell them the story of my adventure.

'Grandad . . . tell us again.'

'You really ate a Kleenex?'

I could have spent my year in Paris avoiding the problem. I could have pretended it wasn't there. I could have gone to Pigalle via Pontoise. But no. I took the bull by the horns. I am now a driver *étoile*. Bravo, Michael. Have another egg. And another cognac.

I turned to look back at the stage behind me on which the eternal tussle continued, and I was struck by a vision. In the middle of Paris, at the very heart of the country, there is this vast, monumental, open space, the majestic epicentre of a breathtaking geometrical architectural vision. And each and every day, this perfectly proportioned, symmetrical centre of the hexagon which is France is transformed into an allegory which proclaims to the rest of the world the major contribution of the nation to Western civilisation: *le bordel*.

Chaos.

8

My first *dîner en ville* had not been an outright success. I had mislaid the digicode, arrived with an unkempt bunch of tinkerbells, and chased after the conversation all evening. I was sure I had left a bad impression. I was therefore surprised to get a call.

'*Monsieur Sadler?*'

It was a woman's voice. Pleasure and grammar do not, as I was much later to discover, make the best bedfellows and I found it difficult to identify myself.

'*Er . . . Oui, c'est moi.*'

Which sounded uncouth. The French, in this instance, would practise linguistic schizophrenia: '*Oui, c'est lui-même.*'

The voice identified herself. Her name was Edith. Edith Delluc. The name didn't immediately ring a bell. I quickly sifted through the visiting cards in my mind but couldn't find either a Madame or a Monsieur Delluc.

'You don't remember me?' she teased.

I hesitated for a moment before adopting a French solution.

'Of course I do.'

You might assume from this that I think the French are outright greasers and the British paragons of honesty. Not at all. Where the Englishman might have the inelegance to confess his lack of education, the French have the elegance to conceal theirs. I had clearly chosen my camp. The dinner – *une petite soirée informelle* – was planned for next Thursday.

Monsieur and Madame Delluc, or Madame Delluc and her lover, or Madame Delluc by herself – although I am convinced I heard a 'we' – *nous serions ravis* – live on rue Gounod in the 17th.

'And this time, Monsieur Sadler, don't forget the code!'
There was a playful lilt in her voice. I blushed.

Where exactly was the rue Gounod? *Paris/Banlieue* pp. 32–33: J4. The best route? Via the Etoile! The Etoile? *Bagatelle!* Peanuts.

Thursday at 20.15 I arrived, *très cool*, at the top of the Avenue Marceau, jumped the lights, drove straight into the traffic, crossed the *place* diagonally, greeting in passing the Xanthia and the pale masons who were still at it, and, taking great care not to singe the metallic finish of the Mazda on the flame on the tomb of the Unknown Warrior, passed right under the Arc de Triomphe and out the other side. *Et vlan!*

Small windproof bouquet and digicode in hand, I arrived at the imposing double doors of the Delluc apartment at the appointed hour. The door was opened by a stocky woman in black. I can't say that I recognised Madame Delluc immediately, but to conceal any hesitation I presented her with the flowers. She looked taken aback, understandably when the real Madame Delluc, whom I did recognise as the ebullient brunette from the Bastille, appeared from the doors giving on to the reception rooms and took the bouquet from the hands of her maid.

'Thank you so much, Madame de Souza.'
Bad start. She must find me *tarte* or *plouc*.

Edith Delluc was extremely elegant, wearing a black sheath dress, and heavy gold jewellery on very delicate neck and wrists. Her mouth was full and dark, a sardonic smile always ready to lighten its corners. It came back to me. Chez Bernard Dubost she was with the publisher, Jean-Damien Prince. The real Monsieur Delluc, to whom she introduces me in the salon, is much older. In fact at the beginning of the evening I thought he was her father, but when we stood to sit around the dining table I saw his hand delicately brush the satin of her waist with a gesture which was far from paternal.

The flat was immense, the ceilings so high that even the furniture, a very imposing collection of chunky *meubles Empire* – chairs and settees dressed up like admirals of the fleet with crests, braid and tassles – looked surprisingly small. On the wall hung tapestries depicting *des scènes galantes* – 'love scenes' – young ladies in Laura Ashley wooed in the middle of flocks of disapproving unicorns. I sipped a glass of insipid port in front of a dark painting in which two Greek hoods wearing legionnaires' underpants were attempting to hide the contents of a Renaissance registered letter from a third thug, the spitting image of Monsieur Rossi minus the braces, who was squatting on a cloud holding a very sharp bolt of lightning.

In the midst of such splendour the conversation seemed trite. Two wives, who discovered they lived in the same *quartier* (*tiens! c'est pas vrai!*), had come across a wonderful new baker and went overboard about his baguette. Elie-Charles, a retired businessman, kept his own boredom at bay by playing golf and guaranteed ours by telling us about it. A wholesaler in upmarket combs and shaving brushes whose passion was car rallies in the desert, told us of a close shave (haha) with a Porsche in Marrakech. A disenchanted industrialist lamanted the decline of the West while his wife got smashed on Martinis. The girlfriend of a sharp-toothed *fonctionnaire* worked in the *cabinet* of a minister. We scrutinised a photo in *Paris Match* of the aforesaid minister on a visit to a jazz club run by the long-term unemployed in Besançon. Was that her in pink behind the trombone? No, it was a geranium. I note we are thirteen at table. Curious. On the menu, parma ham and melon, monkfish accompanied by rice served in a round mould that made it look like a pallid halo, and red fruit and cream – and . . .

'A surprise for Mr Sadler,' says the *maîtresse de maison*. Roland Delluc served the wine decanted. He had a glint in his eye. We had to guess what it was. He was obviously enjoying himself. The assembled palates were mystified. Was it a Bordeaux, a Burgundy? A Côte Rôtie even? Roland chuckled with glee. No one knew. He was delighted with himself and his mystery booze. He shouldn't have been. His wine tasted of old rugs and chocolate.

I was struck by a thought. When they're young, the French drink young wines: these are the gamay days when life is light and fruity. When they're older they buy more mature wines, as rich and wooded as the sentiments they now profess to. This is the era of the cabernet franc and the pinot noir. It's when they age that the worm enters the fruit. When they are old, or as old as Delluc, they have to drink up the wines they laid down when the world seemed bottomless. With the result that they serve elderly booze, decrepit beverages, puffed, thin-blooded and feeble. What was it? A '56 Pontet-Canet? My my, Roland. Could have been Ribena.

After the cheese, a rather juicy camembert which ran up my knife and which the cholesterol brigade shunned like the plague, Edith Delluc stood to go to the kitchen and then stopped at the door: 'Michael, would you give me a hand?'

After several kilometres of corridor we arrived in the depths of the flat. Oddly, as we moved deep into the apartment, we seemed to go back in time. The wallpaper was less chic, the doors less smart. The kitchen was vast, green and appeared to have stepped straight out of a 1950s *Homes and Gardens*. Edith stooped elegantly in her tight black dress to open the oven door.

'*Regardez*, Michael. Especially for you. *Un crumble!*'

A crumble! My grandmother Maud had stuffed me with crumbles from the age of seven to eleven. I would have much preferred a tart or a soufflé. But I was not

going to disappoint a svelte Parisienne out to surprise
me.

'*C'est chaud!* Pass me the plate, Michael.'

Madame de Souza, now wearing an apron to warn off
eventual flower-presenters, could have leapt to her side
but it was me she wanted. I took the porcelain plate –
doubtless Limoges, but this was hardly the moment to
peek at the hallmark – and was at her side in a trice.
Edith had the crumble – '*le crumbelle*' – in her left hand
which was ensconced in an oven glove. She went to take
the Limoges plate from me by slipping her right hand under
the dish. Inevitably our fingertips met. They met because the
plate had to be supported. But they met for longer than it
takes to manoeuvre a crumble into a sliding position. They
touched, they grazed, they lingered, they dallied under the
dish. She could have retracted her fingers. I could have
done the same. Neither of us moved. The moment was
ephemeral but highly charged, erotic. Was this a pass? *Me
drague-t-elle?* I was delightfully troubled.

'Careful, Michael. It's 'ot.'

You can say that again. She smiled. I smiled. Madame
de Souza, who must by now be wondering what was going
on under the dish, coughed. I recovered my senses and the
crumble and enquired about spoons.

'*Il nous faut des cuillères, Edith.*'

'*Cuill-ères*'. Very difficult to pronounce. Edith coached
me. Her rich, deep mouth composed an exaggerated heart
shape as she corrected my accent. Electrified, I walked
back up the corridor from the wings to the stage. I left
the dining room a mere boy, I returned a character from
Les Liaisons dangereuses. I am the Marquis de Valmont,
the John Malkovich of the crumble.

It was on my return that the whole tone of the evening
changed. Either because of the amount of liquid carpet we
had been drinking, or simply by tradition, all the guests,
once the dessert arrived, began to talk *cul* – literally 'arse'

but, part for the whole, normally 'sex'. The transition was as abrupt as if we had changed items on an agenda. We now move on to Any Other Dirty Business. The topic in question was *l'amitié*. Is friendship possible between the sexes?

Elie-Charles put his niblick on his plate and opined.

'Friendship, or at least what I understand by friendship, is strictly impossible between a man and a woman.'

'For once I am in wholehearted agreement,' said his neighbour, the owner of a factory in Brittany which made industrial sponge cakes.

Edith refused to understand.

'*Messieurs!* You are talking nonsense. *Des balivernes!*'

I noted the word.

Elie-Charles lifted a fleshy finger.

'Attention. I hold that friendship between a man and woman is only possible after penetration.'

The sponge cake was even more keen to cross the t's.

'*Distinguo!* After orgasm. True friendship between the sexes is only possible after orgasm.'

Mrs Martini passed me the plate.

'*Encore quelques fruits rouges?*'

'*Avec joie.*'

The French, I am discovering, adore to sit fully clothed around a table and talk about what they do naked in bed. As, I am sure, they adore to talk naked in bed about what they do around a table.

Roland Delluc, even more Olympian than Dédé l'asperge himself, added from the touchline, 'We are talking of course of the calm that follows the storm . . .'

The golfer did a hole in one.

'Let it be said once and for all' – the rhetorical flourish is always present even in matters of *cul* – 'real friendship between a man and woman is only possible in the seven minutes which follow ejaculation.'

The ladies clucked, at once delighted and horrified. Edith seemed to take all this very seriously.

'You are all appallingly macho!'

'*Edith, non. Calme-toi* – you know full well . . .'

'I am not at all in agreement,' she replied. 'Such friendship is quite possible. What do you think, Michael?'

My fingers and mind were still tingling from the crumble encounter and I was not quite sure what to reply. The sponge cake came to my assistance.

'There are two kinds of friendship. Pre-friendship and post-friendship. And the former dwells indubitably in the shadow of an undeclared sensuality.'

'*Mais non!*'

'*Mais si!*'

Edith stood, her eyes afire. She is small, slight, muscular and very beautiful. There are dimples at the tops of her arms as she gesticulates. She points at me.

'Michael needs a guide in his discovery of France.'

'Oh really?' said the sponge cake, eyeing the hostess with some disbelief.

'And I can tell you here and now that I am quite able to be Mr Sadler's friend without there ever being any question either of orgasm or penetration between us.'

'*Chiche*,' said Roland.

Chiche? What did he mean? I had some *pois chiche* with the couscous chez Ali. Why was Roland suddenly talking of chickpeas? The evening ended in a whirlwind of innuendo and double entendre. Then the curtain came down and we were outside on the elegant pavement for the ritual exchange of visiting cards.

As soon as I got home I threw myself on *Le Petit Robert*.

Chiche! interj. fam. 1866. A nineteenth-century familiar interjection: *exclamation de défi*. Expressing a challenge. I'll take you up on it! *Je vous prends au mot. Tu n'oserais jamais – Chiche.* You'd never dare. *Chiche.*

Challenge? What challenge?

9

Elle magazine tells us that the 6th *arrondissement* is a village. What's this, I'd thought. Some arty-farty journalist pretending that Poilâne is the local baker and the Place Sulpice the village square. I was wrong. In many ways the 6th is as chummy as Abesbury. Take shopping, for example.

A Thursday. Got up and went into the lurid, buttercup-yellow kitchen which had been recently redecorated after a flood – *un dégât des eaux* – caused by Monsieur Bandol the retired SNCF railwayman who lives above. Monsieur Bandol is round and squat and looks like a pipe-smoking pear with a beard. He adores *la culture*. Culture, the French are given to saying, is like jam; the less you have, the more you spread it out. This is not the case with Monsieur Bandol. He sees everything at the Comédie Française and has a subscription to the very bulky *Connaissance des arts* which falls on my foot once a month when I open the box for the *plis volumineux*. He has also a prodigious memory. He learned an extraordinary amount of poetry off by heart at school and unfortunately has forgotten none of it. When I go down in the morning to fetch my mail he is waiting for me, ready to unload his hard disk of several kilos of verse. Last week there was a storm while I was trying to decipher my EDF electricity bill. We were plunged into pitch darkness. The hallway was illuminated by intermittent flashes of lightning. Monsieur Bandol adopted the pose of Hernani, the eponymous hero of Hugo's Romantic play, and, holding in his left hand a flier vaunting the merits of

Paul Prédault's ham on the bone – a reasonable description
of his thespian potential – declaimed:

> *Je suis une force qui va!*
> *Agent aveugle et sourd de mystères funèbres!*
> *Une âme de malheur faite avec des ténèbres!*
> *Où vais-je? Je ne sais. Mais je me sens poussé*
> *D'un souffle impétueux, d'un destin insensé.*
> *Je descends, je descends, et jamais je ne m'arrête.*
> (I am a force which moves!
> The blind and heedless agent of mournful mystery
> An ill bent soul cut from the cloth of darkness
> Where am I going? I know not. But I feel impelled
> By some mysterious wind, by some insane destiny.
> I go down, I go down and never shall I stop.)

He would doubtless never have stopped if, at that precise moment, the electricity hadn't come back on. Bandol
changed tack immediately.

'*Et Dieu dit: que la lumière soit. Et la lumière fut!*'

Genesis being less wordy than Hugo, Bandol came to
the end of his recital and I continued to decipher my bill.
Just before I moved in Bandol had been to see Verdi's
Nabucco at the Opéra, forgotten to switch the tap off and
the flood had occurred during the slaves' chorus. The decorator had papered the walls upside-down and the pattern
of Grecian urns against a buttercup-yellow background is
both a reminder of the cause of the redecoration and an
explanation of why I make my coffee wearing sunglasses.

It was thus in a blue towelling bathrobe with my Ray-Bans
on my nose that I opened the fridge to discover that I only
had a couple of spoonfuls of Lavazza in the bottom of
the packet. There was no bread and the *lait demi écrémé*
had gone off. There was a Post-it stuck to the door of
the fridge: buy stamps. Nothing for it. I'd have to go
shopping.

Nine-fifteen, rue du Cherche-Midi. A mere hundred yards to negotiate.

Pretending to be interested in a spot on my nose, I tried to slip past the café without being recognised. The Balto was as difficult to negotiate as the merguez trap chez Ali. L'Asperge, ever vigilant behind the counter, can spot an Englishman engaged in fictitious scratching at fifty metres: '*Salut, Monsieur Mike.*'

I didn't want to jeopardise my new-found friendship. So I had an espresso at the bar – *un petit noir sur le zinc* – in the time it takes to discuss the headlines of *Le Figaro*. The British are apparently refusing to stop using pounds and ounces.

'*Ça pèse combien, une ounce?*' asks Dédé.

I measured out what I guess to be an ounce of sugar on my saucer. Three *croissants beurre* and a *tartine* gathered around to finger it unimpressed.

'*S'énerver pour si peu.*'

I left the Balto, invigorated after *le petit noir*, and crossed over. The menu at the Bar-Tabac des Sports has been unchanged ever since I arrived: *côte de porc charcutière* – a rather tacky sauce with gherkins – *sand wigs*, which I presumed weren't what they said, and the enigmatic *Steck frites*. *Teck* is teek. *Steck* must be meat used to make boats. I only used the Bar des Sports for stamps.

Robert, the patron, is a preserve. As from nine o'clock in the morning he is pickled in alcohol. But, like a prisoner in a minute medieval torture cell, he can't fall over because – by a quirk of fate – he's kept in an upright position by the bar.

'*Un carnet de timbres, s'il vous plaît.*'

Robert serves me an *express*. I always forget. The amount of booze in his head causes his neurons to short-circuit. He suffers from waiter's dyslexia. You order a pastis, he'll serve you a kir. You want a beer, you'll get a Pernod. The next time I want some stamps I'll order a coffee.

I put the money on the counter. Robert, immediately and

with immense pleasure, waves his red-veined finger in front
of my nose as if it was a windscreen-wiper.

'*Non!*'

Robert has acne. There are as many knobs on his face as
in the Concorde cockpit. There's one that lights up when
he's thinking, one that goes off when he's tired, one for
turning right, one for turning left. At the present moment
his face is on Red Alert.

'You haven't got any stamps?'

'*Des timbres? Si!* Of course I've got stamps. But. That's
not enough. *Pas assez!*'

Robert is the Nostradamus of the price rise. He loves
announcing disasters. Five francs on a packet of Marlboro,
twenty centimes on petrol make his day.

'*Qu'est-ce qu'ils nous fabriquent maintenant?*'

What indeed were the evil 'they' concocting to make our
lives even more unliveable? Turning this question over in
my mind, I crossed back over to buy my bottle of Candia
lait frais pasteurisé demi-écrémé. Easier said than done.
Madame Martine loves a conversation. In front of me in
the queue are a kilo of apples, a packet of frankfurters,
two lettuces *sous blister* and a bottle of Côtes-du-Rhône.
Four clients for Martine make a salon. She ought to have
been born in the seventeenth century. She is the Madame
Récamier of the check-out. Before extricating myself from
the shop we go through a broken hip, two dodgy livers and
a divorce. The milk is about to go off.

Once freed, I glimpse Jean-Pierre Goujon's white apron
in the middle distance. I seek refuge in the first shop which
turns out to be the *triperie* and find myself face to face with
a veal's head and surrounded by assorted kidneys, lungs
and udders. The *tripier* and I enjoy a somewhat strained
relationship. His business has been affected by BSE and he
seems to hold me partially responsible. To humour him I
often buy a courtesy kidney. But I haven't had breakfast
and the display of innards makes me feel a little queasy.

I squint and point to the nearest article, which turns out to be a snout – *délicieux, le groin!* – and leave as quickly as possible. A little further up the road I can see the SFR mobile phone shop man waiting for me to see if I have found a penfriend for his son Benoît, fourteen, who likes football, rap, big girls and dope. I turn on my heels. I'm never going to get home.

I beat a retreat via the rue Saint-Placide. I know more people in tripe than in the rag trade and the street – in which Joris Karl Huysmans, the author of the decadent *A Rebours*, once lived – is now just one big clothes shop. At the top, just after the bank, and a right turn into the rue de Vaugirard, there's an extraordinary no-man's-land, a good twenty metres without a shop or a café. No one to stop me for a chat.

Famous last words. With a jaunty spring in his step, Monsieur Bandol is advancing towards me in his bright red shoes. He has just seen *Cyrano de Bergerac* for the fifth time. I can see what is going to happen. He's going to nail me on the corner and give me the famous Nose monologue: '*C'est un roc! . . . c'est un pic! C'est un cap! Que dis-je, c'est un cap? . . . C'est une péninsule.*'

I duck into the entrance of the *lycée technique* and contemplate the results of last year's examinations for the *tourneurs fraiseurs* – strawberry turners?

I arrive back home at ten past eleven. Stamps, milk, coffee and snout. Job done. Only it's too late for breakfast. I'll have to go back down again to buy lunch.

10

Tourneur fraiseur means a machine operator. *Une fraise*, as well as a strawberry, is a drill.

French has become a tricky language. In the Baroque sixteenth century it was every man for himself. Rules were not the flavour of the month. Montaigne's spelling was almost as idiosyncratic as my own. But in the classical seventeenth century, the 'linguistically correct' entered the arena. The kings, Louis XIII and particularly XIV, aided and abetted by the *éminence grise* himself, Cardinal Richelieu, decided to centralise the country and, to that effect, started to impose upon France the dialect of the Ile de France as *the* national French language. If everyone spoke the same they ought to be less bolshie and more governable. Regional languages – the *oc* and the *oïl* in particular – were outlawed. French was thus enriched at the same time as it was impoverished – there are some 300,000 words in the French dictionary, more than three times that number in the English. This new lingo was as complex as the rules of the court which used it. It was and still is an aristocratic language – look in a *Petit Larousse*. You'll find a lot of words for the different parts of a nobleman's hunting saddle but only one for a puddle – *une flaque*.

So it happened that official French, under the aegis of the newly born Académie Française (1636), became a headache, even for the French themselves. In the literary *salons*, in the *ruelles* – the space between bed and wall where the artists presented their work – at the *lever* and *coucher* of the King – the ceremonial goings-to-bed and gettings-up – the French-speaker was hedged in by rules and regulations. He could no longer say, '*J'ai paumé mes brodequins*' ('I've lost my shoes') because you couldn't name things, for fear of being branded vulgar. He would have to say something more like, '*Quel esprit malin a fait disparaître mes enveloppes pédestres?*' ('What evil spirit has caused my pedestrian envelopes to disappear?'). If you didn't know how to handle the imperfect subjunctive, you were out on your nose. What a bumpkin! *Quelle patate* (what a spud!). They would split their doublets laughing. There was, of course, resistance in the provinces. So much so that, until the arrival on the scene of minister of education Jules Ferry at the end of the nineteenth century, who instituted free state education for all, most of France didn't speak French.

There are those who believe that the French spend their time inventing difficulties just to make life impossible for foreigners. Take, for example, the most infamous grammar of all, *Le Bon Usage*, by Maurice Grevisse (published by Monsieur Duculot, whose name means 'what a nerve!'). *Le Bon Usage* is the Mrs Beeton of linguistic nightmares.

Open it at random – page 234, article 291: the plural of composite nouns.

'Composite nouns which are written as ordinary nouns form their plural in the normal way: passport for instance – *un passeport, des passeports*.'

Don't worry. It's not as simple as that.

'When composite nouns are formed by the combination of two co-ordinated nouns, then the two nouns carry the mark of the plural: e.g. county town – *un chef-lieu*, therefore *des chefs-lieux*.' Or, a bayonet/sabre – *un sabre-baïonnette* – gives *des sabres-baïonnettes*. Extremely useful if you want to say: 'I lost many bayonet sabres in just as many county towns.' Porcupine follows the same rule: *des porcs-épics*. Doubtless because they could be mistaken for the *sabres-baïonnettes*. But the Academy is none too sure if this rule holds for all nouns – for instance: *pince-monseigneur* – a jemmy. No one seems sure of what the plural of jemmy is. How awful. Think of the heart-searching this could cause amongst gentlemen-burglars. Come to think of it, what's the plural of *gentleman-cambrioleur?* This reflexion upon compound plurals continues for the next twelve pages, which might explain why French is such a singular language.

Everyday I subject myself to a linguistic discipline. I try to read the daily paper *Libération*. Sitting on the floor in the shadow of my green plant, with the Collins Robert bilingual dictionary, some black olives and a *petite récolte* from Nicolas, I set about cracking the political pages. No mean task. Wednesday's text reads as follows: '*Issu du sérail, Antoine Gaudron, qui a toujours fait partie du peloton de tête, a, à son corps défendant, mis le feu aux poudres en découvrant le pot aux roses.*'

Thirty words. Hardly a day's grind you might say. Then have a go yourself. What exactly was he up to, the Monsieur Gaudron in question? None too easy to say. With the assistance of the dictionary I managed to unravel the following: 'Born in a harem, Anthony Gaudron, who had always been an excellent cyclist, became a pyromaniac in spite of himself when he came across the flowerpot.'

Libé costs 7 francs. Quite expensive for gibberish.

I consulted the brains of the Balto, my local Académie Française, and eventually cracked it. I had omitted to take into account the intensely metaphorical nature of French. This is what I should have understood: 'Monsieur Gaudron, who is part of the political establishment and who has always been a leading figure in the public eye, unintentionally put the cat amongst the pigeons when he stumbled on the secret.'

According to my most recent calculations I will have mastered the language by the year 2084.

11

In Abesbury people are what Parisians would call *mou*. *Mou* in the morning, *mou* in the evening, *mou* at supper time. *Mou*? 'Soft, lethargic, yielding, slack, flaccid, lax, nerveless,' says the dictionary. It's true. We laxly greet our neighbour over the fence, flaccidly comment on the weather and give the dog a nerveless pat. No one complains, no one protests. Life's storms pass us by. No one actually dies in Abesbury. We are merely enveloped in a benign pleat of the soft skirt of eternity.

The Parisian, by way of contrast, is 100 per cent unlax, unflaccid and unslack. Someone is too slow getting out of a taxi? He hangs out of the car, one hand on the horn, the other making gestures which are more appropriate to the last act of *La Traviata* than to the rue du Four. The French are *nerveux* – fast, emotional, Latin. As my first lesson taught me.

Edith Delluc was determined to take my education in hand. She rang me a few days after our dinner, fired by her husband's *chiche*. We were to start with some of the cultural highspots of the capital. A rendezvous was fixed for the following Tuesday in a brasserie on the Boulevard Saint-Germain, Chez Lipp. I presumed that we would then be off to visit the Panthéon, the Conciergerie or the Louvre.

As always I arrived early. There is undoubtedly something *plouc* about punctuality. No one *chic* I have ever met arrives on time. Not keeping people waiting is a sign of an attention and a generosity to others that is somehow unbecoming. Too bad. I entered the brasserie through the revolving door and found myself in an attractive old-world Parisian restaurant with ceramic tiles of exotic plants on the walls and vast mirrors at slanted angles. Everyone looked up to see who I might be and looked down again when they saw I wasn't. Edith Delluc of course hadn't arrived. Fortunately a waiter – long white apron, black waistcoat, white shirt, black bow tie – came to my aid. His eyes asked the question: was I expecting someone? I nodded, he smiled, accompanied me to the foot of the staircase, and gestured for me to go up.

The upstairs room was light and empty with a most attractive view over the Boulevard Saint Germain. A perfect place to keep a rendezvous. I sat and happily watched Paris going by. Buses, jams, girls, tourists, Les Deux Magots and the Café Flore opposite, buses, jams, cars, girls . . .

Still no Edith. I began to wonder whether I had not misunderstood the day of the week when, some twenty-four minutes later (Edith was now eighteen minutes late) the *garçon* who had so kindly shown me upstairs reappeared with his tail very much between his legs. He looked abashed, crestfallen, sheepish, embarrassed or, if you prefer, *penaud, déconcerté, désemparé, démonté, confondu, consterné, décontenancé, déconfit, interdit, pantois, désarçonné, camus* (*Larousse Dictionary of Synonyms*, p. 181).

'Madame Delluc is waiting for you, Monsieur. She . . . requests me to ask you to come downstairs,' he mumbled.

Odd. Why didn't she come up herself? I followed the waiter back down into the busy restaurant area. Edith was sitting at a table looking furious. Before I could open my mouth she asked, 'What were you doing up there, Michael?!'

I started to explain the considerable advantages of the upstairs room – its airiness, the view, the calm . . . She interrupted me. Her tone was dry and scornful.

'You could have waited for me a long time.'

I didn't understand.

'Listen, Michael . . . Let this be your first lesson. No one, understand me, *no one* ever goes upstairs Chez Lipp.'

Unless of course you are a Lithuanian tourist or an English academic.

Edith nodded to the waiter who was eyeing us from a safe distance.

'Georges.'

And Georges disappeared, to reappear almost immediately with two *coupes de champagne*.

'Georges wants to apologise.'

'*Excusez-moi, Monsieur. Si j'avais su que vous attendiez Madame Delluc . . . évidemment . . .*'

'*Non . . . er . . . Georges. Ce n'est rien.*' Think nothing of it, my man.

Edith seemed less inclined to excuse and asked for another *coupe*. She set about explaining the nature of my crime. She spoke fast, half in French, half in English. It was the French that I understood best. The gist of the whirlwind was the following. If I am to live in Paris I must know how to behave. Otherwise I might as well stay in Tunbridge Wells, *n'est-ce pas?* Edith lowered her voice. The cultural highspot she wanted to introduce me to was not the Musée d'Orsay, it was . . . Chez Lipp! Clearly I had no idea where I was. *Quand même!* Chez Lipp is no ordinary brasserie. Lipp has been an institution since it was founded in 1880 by Léonard Lipp. Chez Lipp is the Medicis' court. Verlaine, Proust, Gide, Hemingway used to come here. Lipp is the select meeting-place of politicians, of men of letters, lawyers, media moguls, of the great and powerful. It is here that reputations are made and undone. Here that presidents Pompidou, Giscard d'Estaing and Mitterrand would come for a late night *cervelas rémoulade* and *pied de porc*. Here that Bernard Pivot brings his literary guests after the late Friday night show. And I went upstairs?

I went red.

Lipp, she continued passionately, her eyes afire, is not a

café. It is a minefield. One foot out of place and you're finished. Boom, exploded, shrapnel. The utmost care is called for. It is vital not to make a mistake. Edith took a piece of paper and a Bic pen and drew a plan of the restaurant. We are in the main room. The throne room. This room is called *Le Paradis*. Did I get it? It is here that you can see and be seen. The slanted mirrors allow for total vision. I asked if periscopes were also provided but she told me to shut up, tapping me on the knuckles with the pen. The same knuckles she had caressed under the crumble.

'*Je suis sérieuse . . .*'

To the left of the throne room there is a small passageway leading to a back room near the kitchen. This is known as Purgatory. You are given a table in Limbo until your career, charisma or contacts allow you to enter Paradise. But no one – *je répète, personne!* – no one ever goes upstairs. It is the Gobi desert. Known amongst the *Lippistes* as *l'enfer*. Hell.

I suppose, all in all, Edith was giving me a bit of her Lipp. I was chastened. No easy job being a Parisian.

12

The twenty-seventh of November. Le Big Day at last. The Famous Five arranged to meet at the Balto chez Dédé l'Asperge. As soon as I entered I sensed the atmosphere of solemnity. This was not an occasion to be taken lightly. Everyone was wearing ties. Today everyone, I noted, called Dédé *président*.

'*Bonjour président. Ca va-t-y?*'

And Dédé addressed us all as *messieurs*: '*Un Alexandra, messieurs?*'

He was to give me the recipe later, carefully copied out on to the block of squared paper he used to take orders in the café wearing his gold-rimmed half-moon glasses. I had it framed: 'Put the ice cubes in the shaker; add six soup-spoonfuls of cognac, six of *crème de cacao* and the same amount of fresh cream. Shake rapidly to prevent the ice melting. Pour through a sieve into cocktail glasses. Add whipped cream to the surface of the liquid. Drink langorously.'

The advantage of an Alexandra is that it numbs you to any alarm its contents might cause. After three of them – '*messieurs*, a little self-control' said Dédé as we were contemplating a fourth – the Club attacked the rue du Cherche-Midi which, normally pretty straight, suddenly seemed more sinuous. We were heading for the wood-fronted, wine-coloured Nicolas store which is opposite Didier's deep-sea-blue fish shop. Francis opened the door – it is closed all day Monday. The bottles on the shelves jumped to attention as we passed. The whole place smelled of wine and wood.

In a smallish back store room surrounded by boxes and crates, a trestle table covered by a large white tablecloth had been set up. In one corner of the room a plastic protective sheet – the kind you might put over your car to prevent pigeons redecorating it – had been removed from a small gas cooker which the Club bought three years ago from the domestic appliances megastore Darty. A display model at the knockdown price of 850 francs. Francis immediately served a white wine from the Jura – an Arbois – to put us back on our feet after the journey from the Balto. The wine was too cold – *trop frappé* – but if you held the glass in the cup of your hand to warm its bottom you could apparently release the aromas of nuts and lilies. My tastebuds were in a state of post-Alexandra euphoria and if he had told me his wine tasted of rabbits and prunes I would equally have believed him. Lucien Goujon took his jacket off.

'Messieurs. *Aux choses sérieuses* . . . Down to work.'

To tickle our appetite which, according to Didier, must rise to the surface like a pike to its bait, rich, soft, deep-brown rillettes are served on thick toasted, garlic-rubbed chunks of Poilâne bread from just down the road. A third bottle of Arbois hits the deck. We were cleaning our palates – '*Nous éclaircissons nos palais*,' said Francis, in case anyone might suspect us of drinking.

An extraordinarily mouth-watering smell of grilled meat came from inside the Darty cooker. We sat around the table. Guest of honour, I was on the left of President Dédé. Lucien Goujon, his back turned at the oven, suddenly presented me with a vast white plate on which sizzled grilled . . . I wasn't sure quite what. The Arbois, while it got my pike to rise, had somewhat impaired my vision. It was dead, it was meat, it was grilled. But what was it?

'*Des oreilles*, Michael.'

Ears?!

Jean-Claude gave me a torturer's smile.

'*Des oreilles de cochon!*'

Pigs' ears, severed from the head, slowly simmered over-night by the *charcutier* in the broth in which he cooks the trotters and the York ham, then seared under the grill. Ears which, now I came to focus on them, did, yes, look extraordinarily like ears. The kind of pink floppy jobs that curl over in a winsome way on dogs or other chummy animals. The Club looked at me in an attentive, quizzical silence. Jean-Claude, in particular, wanted to put me to the test. Would I or wouldn't I? Faced with a pig's appendages, would the *rosbif* chicken out?

I hesitated. National pride was at stake. I brought the ear ceremoniously to my mouth and slowly sank my teeth into the fleshy lobe. The texture was soft and cartilaginous, gelatinous and resistant. I chewed, I masticated, I savoured. The Club was agog. *Alors?*

'*Le Paradis!*'

It was heaven. The quintessence of pig. A pork nirvana. My friends were delighted and relieved. They had been right to invite me. I had passed the test. I was one of them. They exchanged approving glances, apart from Jean-Claude, who seemed miffed that I hadn't passed out. To reward me for my courage the Club awarded me a second ear.

But the pig was only an appetiser. The main dish – the *plat de résistance* – belonged to that category of 'forbidden food' they had whispered to me about. The menu of their lunches was never broadcast in advance. They were top secret. For their mouths only. The president rose to his feet and took a large serving dish which had been delicately balancing on top of a row of bottles in the shop's wine cooler. It was covered by a white cloth. With the stage presence of a magician, Dédé put one hand on the edge of the cloth and slowly revealed the majesty of what was beneath.

'*Messieurs. Je vous présente. Les tabliers de sapeur!*'

Applause.

After the auditory organs of the pig, firemen's aprons?

The room was as silent as a church. The high priest continued and his prophesy enlightened us to the imminent delight.

'You take the lining of the stomach of the cow. You then cut the thick beige coloured *panse* into triangles which you then proceed to cook for two hours in a *court bouillon* composed of water, white wine, carrots, onions, *bouquet garni*. You then remove the triangles, dry them on absorbent paper and prepare the *panage*: they are dipped in flour, then in eggs beaten with mustard, white wine, salt and pepper, then finally in the breadcrumbs, homemade from lovingly dried and crumbled wholemeal bread. Not Poilâne, it is too lumpy.'

The congregation was bewitched and watched in silence as Dédé rose, went to the altar and set about frying the aprons. He lifted them to the air and placed them with loving care in the hot fat. We stood alongside, attentive, *officiants* at this gluttonous Mass. The contents of the pan were renewed several times to prevent the taste of rancid burning. Three packets of butter and half a litre of olive oil were necessary for the operation to succeed.

When the aprons were fried taut they were presented on the serving dish with chunks of lemon and sprinkled with crudely chopped flat – not curly – parsley. Lucien then whipped another dish from the oven: '*Messieurs. Le gratin dauphinois.*'

The acolytes were in seventh heaven.

'*C'est trop, c'est trop, Lucien . . .*'

But it wasn't too much. The vast earthenware dish in which several kilos of golden-fleshed waxy Charlotte potatoes had spent the morning slowly cooking in cream, garlic and nutmeg was emptied in no time.

'*C'est trois étoiles, l'Asperge! Trois étoiles!*'

Lunch passed in a haze of delight and Gigondas. The aprons and the *gratin* were followed by a cheese board

– mostly from the Auvergne, Cantal, tomme frâiche, bleu d'Auverge, St-Nectaire, followed by an apricot and coconut *tarte tatin* – the upside-down tart with its caramelised fruit top – coffee, marc de Bourgogne, coffee, marc de Bourgogne.

The subjects of conversation? First politics. Dangerous ground. Fishmonger and photocopier, in disagreement about the *cohabitation*, were on the point of coming to blows. Dédé, ever wise, called them to order.

'*Messieurs . . . du calme . . .*'

And he brought out a secret bottle *de derrière les fagots* – a mellow, amber, venerable Vouvray *moelleux* which tempered the heated minds. This was his famous *vin de défâchement* – his pipe of peace. And with the Vouvray we talked sex. A magic combination. What politics divided, sex united. We bonded, debonded, rebonded. I learned a new word for a woman – *une gonzesse* – which I'm longing to use at a cocktail party – *permettez moi de vous présenter ma gonzesse* – but I'm not sure the register is correct. My temerity well stoked by the Côtes-du-Rhône, I decided to tell a story in order to thank my new friends for the honour they were doing me.

'Friday morning, on the market boulevard Raspail, I kept losing my trousers. Not that I'd lost weight. On the contrary. But I'd left my belt on another pair of trousers that I'd anointed with *bœuf bourguignon* in a moment of distraction.'

(I have to add that I didn't say *ceinture* – belt – because out of nowhere, my lexical unconscious unleashed by the wine, I said *laiches*, the word I'd learned in Dieppe for the Livarot hernia rushes. No one understood. I resubsituted *ceinture*.)

'So I kept hitching up my trousers. This annoyed Monsieur Seguy, whose guinea fowl were the delights of my Sunday evenings. He took his knife and cut me a length of thread, telling me it was the first time he'd ever used chicken string for a *rosbif*!'

They fell about. Not that the story was so funny but because I was taking the piss out of the English. I was one of them. But I hadn't finished! I'd kept the best for the end. I told them that I'd since found a solution to the trouser problem. I opened my jacket, kept carefully buttoned during the meal, and revealed ... my red, white and blue Union Jack braces presented to me by the village of Abesbury.

'*Ah! Ce sacré Mike!*'

They called me Mike.

And for the first time Lucien Goujon pummelled me.

Lunch broke up at 18.45. Each member of the Club covered his tracks. Didier had been at a meeting at Rungis – the new Halles de Paris. Dédé had *tapé la belote* – which means played cards. In fact I thought he'd said *tapé la belette* which, when I looked it up, meant 'hitting the weasel' which seemed an unnecessarily sadistic alibi. Jean-Claude had been visiting the non-existent National Museum of Photocopying. It was he who stood for the final toast. We raised our glasses.

'*Messieurs. Nous sommes les kamikazes de la bouffe!*'

We were, yes, in a sense a band of suicidal eaters. But I wasn't sure that Jean-Claude included me in the squadron.

13

Take the 95 from the rue de Rennes and head towards the Opéra. The bus goes down the rue Bonaparte across the Pont de Carrousel with the Musée d'Orsay on your left and the Pont des Arts and l'Institut, home of the Académie Française, on your right. It then enters the monumental archway of the Louvre. The bus now drives through what must be one of the world's most magnificent architectural treasures – the majestic three-sided Cour Napoléon, the Pei pyramid, the reflections of the ornate stonework in the marble black water of the pools, the long vista up the Champs-Elysées towards the Arc de Triomphe. What is perhaps even more remarkable than the view is that nobody looks at it. In the bus a lady explains the bandage on her finger, a man reads *Le Monde*, two *lycéennes* giggle, others stare into nowhere.

How do they do it? This zen-like ability to be oblivious to beauty is the result of a long process of assimilation. It takes time, practice and concentration. And it is an essential component of the art of being Parisian.

Conscious of the fact that I am still at the Kodak Gold stage of my exploration of the city – my eyes refocus, zoom, compose and click every time I see something that takes my breath away – I decided to explore Paris with the precise aim of taking it for granted.

In the past weeks I have got pretty much used to the majestic Place des Vosges, the romantic Butte aux Cailles, the swish 16th, and Chinatown in the 13th. I have also managed to tame the Jardin du Luxembourg. The Luco, as

I have learned to call it familiarly, is divided into different areas: the games area where old men play chess and eat sandwiches wrapped in aluminium foil packets; the solarium near the *orangerie*, where chic retired ladies expose their skin to holes in the ozone layer; the carousel area, excellent for eyeing up young mothers; the *bassin*, where children and the same young mothers play with toy yachts under the lubricious gaze of senators gazing down on them from the pannelled splendour of their palace; and the Lolita area on the southern extremity near the Lycée Montaigne, full of *jeunes filles en fleurs*. Last Thursday I managed to walk across the Luco without looking at anything. I am making progress.

I was, however, being blasé about the Paris I knew. More dangerous, because it could take me by surprise and reveal that I am still a mere novice, was the Paris I didn't know. So I decided to give chance a chance. I would get on the métro, get off at any old station and walk.

Yesterday I found myself in a little square not far from the rue Rossini. The late afternoon light was golden, there had been a shower and the birds were singing *bel canto* in the trees. I contemplated this Parisian scene with emotion. It was like a Sempé drawing – the square, the prams, the geometric beds of flowers, the statue of DEC..R..S – the plinth with the name was cracked but it looked strangely like Marguerite Duras wearing a wet wig – the hut of the *gardien du square*, the barrow of the leaf sweeper and . . . the *sanisette* Decaux.

The *sanisette* Decaux is a newish protuberance in Parisian street architecture. Public loos in France have been famous since *Clochemerle* and the municipal battle over the ornate iron *vespasienne*, the archetypal French urinal which reveals the legs and the head but hides the essentials – the French, as all users of *routes nationales* in France know, have always been public pissers. They were named after the Roman emperor Vespasian not because he was incontinent but because he was the first to levy a tax on urinals. France has always been famous for its loos since the reported disappearance of several tourists over the years down the infamous *toilettes à la turque*, the foot-soaking, trouser-drenching crouchers which are the bane of the clean-living Anglo-Saxon. The *sanisette* Decaux is a high-tech answer to the Turkish deathtrap. It is reported to be a TGV. A *très grandiose vespasienne*. It is named after Mr Decaux who runs the company which provides free municipal architecture in exchange for advertising space.

The *sanisette* – which, let's face it, is a repulsive word, managing to combine the sanitary with a coy diminutive in *-ette* – looks like a cross between a money box and a tin of spam. It is ugly but it has always fascinated me. How do they open? What are they like inside? Chintz and leather armchairs? I am an intrepid explorer who refuses no challenge. To the weak-hearted among you, may my example be a lesson.

The square was almost empty at this time of the early evening. No one was watching. The moment was propitious. I put my penny in the slot. Loo and behold the machine, instead of rejecting the coins, hummed, swallowed the cash and obligingly opened its sliding door. It was a pushover. With trepidation I went inside. The door closed behind me.

I found myself in an orbital space station. One moment in the square Rossini, the next in Mir. In order to record the moment for posterity I sat on the loo and took out my camera, and narrowly missed being drenched by the automatic flusher. Beware. The Turkish syndrome lives on.

My photograph taken, I decided to curtail my visit – climbers have been known to spend only seconds on the summit of Everest. But I couldn't get out. The door didn't open. In these circumstances I acted as would any sane man. I panicked. My imagination ran riot. Alone, entombed, buried alive in this sanitary coffinette, my memory called to mind the heroes of Nasa. I thought with great sympathy of Virgil Grissom who perished in his space capsule even before the launcher took off. What a fate. To come so far to die suffocated in a tin of spam. My life passed rapidly before my eyes. I viewed with a strange detachment my failures and my achievements. I decided to leave my liver to AA, my olive oil to the lady downstairs who makes the staircase stink of *Végétaline*, my books to Monsieur Bandol and my green plant to the botanic gardens.

At that moment, that almost sensual moment of total surrender to my morbid destiny, a final glimmer of reason and logic illuminated the deepest recess of my brain. There must be a magic eye concealed somewhere in this ultra-modern design. It's just a question of passing your hand through the beam and the door will open just as it did from the outside. Calm, Sadler. I slid my hand under the tap, over the coat peg, in front of the mirror, hoping to find myself once again bathed in the vesperal glow of the square Rossini.

No go. Nothing happened. Perhaps the loo seat was the key to my salvation. What a clever idea. I sat down again. Got drenched. Stood. Nothing. Wet in vain. Sod. I was like Aïda at the end of Verdi's opera, entombed in her mausoleum, without even an Egyptian prince to keep me company. Were these toilets airtight? I could see the head-lines: 'UNIVERSITY TEACHER SUFFOCATES IN DECAUX TOMB'.

A final ray of hope. Just as I was contemplating using the little oxygen remaining to dig a tunnel with my bare hands, I heard the squeak of the leaf sweeper's barrow. Like a miner trapped deep in his pit knocking in Morse on the tracks of the underground railway, I started to tap what I thought should be 'may-day' on the walls of the money box. I heard the sweeper stop. Leave his barrow. He was coming towards the *sanisette*. I am saved! I knock again. But then he knocks back. I knock twice. He knocks twice. The stupid bugger! He thinks it's a game! Tragedy and farce are so often bedfellows. I shouted.

'*Monsieur! Monsieur!* You've got it wrong. *Vous vous trompez!* I am a prisoner of the *sanisette*.'

The sweeper replied. What's he saying? I can't understand a thing. And he can't understand me. I've got an English accent and he's got an African accent. Communication is impossible. He bangs rhythmically on the side of his barrow as he leaves.

'*Salut!*'

Silence falls. I sit down again. To hell with the flusher. The square will soon be closing for the night. After what seems an eternity, I hear steps again. They approach the *sanisette*. An angry voice. A knocking on the coffin lid.

'*Vous vous grouillez oui ou merde!*'

I recognise the angry military tone. It must be a Livarot! My saviour. Kneeling at the door like a virgin at the confessional, I told my awful story.

'I'd love to hurry. But I can't get out!'

'And the handle? *La poignée?* Why not turn it! *Mais quel con!*'

A handle? Why had I never thought of a handle? It never struck me that in my twenty-first-century orbital loo station there would be anything so nineteenth-century as a handle. I find it, turn it, open the door.

As *penaud* as Georges the Lipp *garçon*, I stammered my thanks to my red-faced, incontinent saviour and made my way to the middle of the now-deserted square to sit on the broken stone under the statue of Marguerite Duras, she who knew so much about human torment. Life has become too complex. Existence is fraught with unnecessary danger. In the past such claustrophobia was unthinkable. It was strictly impossible to lock yourself in a *vespasienne*.

14

Over the festive period in England there is a marked increase in internecine murder. This is not surprising. Everything closes for six or seven days and there is nothing left to do but to kill your relatives. Grannies are hung from the paper chains, children stuffed into stockings. In France, which is a Catholic country, everything, on the contrary, is open for business – they don't even close on Good Friday, I was to discover later. Trains run, cafés serve *un petit noir* from the early hours and the mutual extermination graph doesn't signal any significant movement. To be honest, apart from a considerable increase in the daily intake of *boudin blanc*, I hardly saw Christmas go by.

'What are you doing for ze New Yeaar?' Edith Delluc did her Catherine Deneuve imitation down the phone. 'Nozzing? *Parfait*! You 'ave, you just must 'ave to taste what is the *réveillon à la française*.' And she invites me *illico* – a French Latin tag meaning 'there and then' – to spend ze New Year in ze big 'ouse which Roland Delluc owns in Touraine. She announces the programme in advance.

'*On va s'amuser!*'

How did she know we were going to have a good time?

In order to find a present for the Delluc (no 's' on family names in French) I decided to go to the Bon Marché, the chic store just down the road which has recently been done up at great cost. There is, on the second floor of the right-hand building, a lingerie department complete with pink sofas for men to lounge on pretending to be thinking of the *Bourse* or horses as their wives struggle into a number they would never wear if their husbands weren't acting nonchalant outside. The more casual the husband, the naughtier the number. Impossible for me to make the most of the delights of the right-hand store – I could hardly arrive as a house guest bringing a diaphanous *nuisette* as a present – and so I decide to concentrate my researches on the delights of the left-hand store – *la grande épicerie de Paris*.

A wise choice. For the festive period they were organising *la fête des vignerons*. Selected wine growers from all over France are invited to the store, you turn up, proffer your glass, they fill it, you drink it and an hour and half later you climb back up the stairs home on all fours, plastered and enlightened. That, at least, was what I thought.

Let it be said from the outset. I am no amateur. My palate has been formed by the Fruit Wine Society of Abesbury under Lyme. Come October every year in the village hall, a collection of red-cheeked nutters bring a host of extraordinary beverages for you to tipple – wine made from kiwis, rhubarb, fermented elastic bands, pigeon shit, you name it. I arrived in the Bon Marché for the beginning of the week. And what a beginning! Posters announced a vertical tasting of a famous Burgundy. Literally and metaphorically, we were going to down the years '97, '96, '95, '94 etc. At six-fifteen on the dot I was at the electric doors of the *épicerie*, tastebuds akimbo, ready to embark on a vertical that would doubtless leave me horizontal.

The wine department is situated in the back left-hand corner of the store. I was tempted to do a bit of shopping on my way through but . . . not tonight Josephine. Too many old ladies. Too many smart, powdered, beautifully made-up, short elderly Parisians out tonight. Be warned. You stand there in front of the electronic weighing machine, searching in vain for the picture of the vegetable in your plastic bag. The pictograms are not in alphabetical order. You panic because you can feel the intolerant classy hot

Parisian breath of the ladies behind you, their impatience on the hob under their mink stoles. What *are* your beans? Green or coco? Suddenly a crabbed jewelled finger overtakes your hesitant arm. You look round. She's 3 foot 6 high, dripping in pearls and perfume, looking like a stoat off to a cocktail party: '*Trouvé!*'

And bingo. She presses the button. The right one? You're joking. She can't wait, time is short when you've got nothing to do, so she hits any button she can reach in order to get you to move on. Net result. You end up at the cash desk with leeks weighed at the price of truffles.

Large testicular bunches of polystyrene grapes hang down from the high-tech ceiling like props from a bacchic nightmare. When I arrive in the wine department a silent group of tasters has already gathered, like beggars at the door of the monastery, their heads slightly bowed in the direction of a light oak altar on which, standing next to a bottle and twenty-odd glasses neatly aligned on a tray, is the icon which inspires the most profound respect: the price tag. I genuflect in the direction of 229.00FF and humbly take my place in the congregation. Who are they? A mixed bunch. Several retired businessmen with fiery cheeks and the *légion d'honneur*, a cluster of enthusiasts who exchange endless tasting notes as if they were olfactory stamp collectors and a dentist with a nose like a hoover.

The high priest arrives. I had been expecting a kind of rubicond *vigneron*, as plump as a monk on a Livarot box, but this particular one is rather surprising. Thin and pale, besuited and boring, he looks more like a banker – which is not surprising considering the price of his booze. Solemnly he opens the '97 and declares it still closed. First paradox.

The glasses pass from hand to hand. They only contain a dribble of nectar, the merest lark's pee, but, making the most of all situations, *vita brevis*, I down it. I was expecting a floral explosion. Nothing of the sort. The wine remains acid, neutral and poor. But my fellow experts, all united around a silver bowl, are looking at me askance. Could it be that a lush has infiltrated the brotherhood? Second paradox. To drink you have to spit.

Even worse. You have to say what you think of it. The evaluations are uttered in an intelligent undertone . . . 'fat', 'tannic', 'well built'. We are all standing in a row. Inevitably my turn comes. I chicken out.

'Actually it's quite nice.'

Nice? Nice! The palates frown. The high priest gives me a shriveller.

'No, *Monsieur*. In fact it won't even begin to be "nice" for at least fifteen years.'

I make my way immediately to the FNAC – the culture megastore in the rue de Rennes – up to the second floor, books, and I plunge into the Parker, the Bible of Booze. I am, of course, not looking for knowledge. I am looking for revenge. Parker, the biggest wine-buff bluffer of them all, has a palate and a nose like a computer. As I read I begin to twig the system.

Day 2: a tasting of Bordeaux. Bloody but unbowed, I clock in at the oak altar at 6.15. They're all there, the aces of yesterday who sneered at my fulsome innocence. Let them wait and see. The glasses come round, a swill, a taste, a spit. The palates begin their boring litany: body, legs, structure. My turn approaches. I push my nose as far down the glass as it will go, extract it and murmur: 'Interesting . . . but the buttocks a shade on the flabby side, wouldn't you say?'

There is a quivering amongst the *légions d'honneur*.

'In fact, *entre nous*, I'd say a little too much bum.'

Bum?! Hum . . .

Silence falls.

And then a voice from the far left of the church: 'I see what you mean.'

It worked! One of the stamp collectors has fallen for it! All you have to do is to choose a theme, push the metaphor as far as you can go, light the blue touchpaper and retire.

There's always going to be someone thicker than you to swallow it.

The next day: Bordeaux blancs. Theme: golf.

Doubtful, I frown, puckering my palate.

'Still a little in the rough, wouldn't you say?'

They certainly would.

Day 4: the Côte de Nuits. Theme: the automobile. My companions are beginning to hold back until I have pronounced judgement.

'Suspension good. But fires unevenly. A distributor problem perhaps? Either needs a few years or a service.'

To finish triumphantly on the last day with Madiran and sex.

'Titillating preliminaries certainly . . . but ultimately a shade exhibitionist . . . Have you ever tried the '69?'

At the end of the week the group is in agreement. I may have given a bad first impression but . . . *en fin de compte*, my expertise leaves them flabbergasted. Even the dentist is taken in by my buccal bluffing.

'Ah, the English . . . We should never forget! Bordeaux belonged to them!'

For Edith and Roland Delluc I bought a bottle of Condrieu, the only wine, of all those I had drunk during the week, which left even me speechless.

15

New Year's Eve falling on a weekend I decided to leave for Touraine, the playground of kings and court in the seventeenth century, a day early. I wanted to make a pilgrimage.

I used to be the proud owner of a grey Austin Mini whose head gasket was as emotional as an inhabitant of Toulouse confronted with a cassoulet and which blew (off) with similar regularity. One day, the gasket, which until then had shown unusual resilience, choosing not to explode, as it often did, in spots such as Scotch Corner or Watford Gap, decided to give up the ghost at a town called Gacé in the Orne, altitude 196 metres, twenty-seven kilometres from Laigle, i.e., in the middle of nowhere. The garage was efficient, the hotel cheap and clean. It was while I was walking in the town after dinner that I stumbled upon one of those revelations that only a breakdown can bring. In a quiet and dimly lit back street I came across one of the most beautiful window displays of my life. The shop surround was in dark red wood, the name of the owner was in faded gold paint, the refrigerated window was composed of slabs of blue grey marble. And on the slabs carefully set out according to their different sizes were stone pots of tripe. *Tripes à la mode de Caen.*

I stood there transfixed.

Tripes à la mode de Caen are made from three different kinds of *gras double*: the *bonnet*, which looks like the thick beige wool you use for making balaclavas; the *feuillet*, like an elongated pile of sticky banknotes; and the very attractive alveolated *nid d'abeille*, the only one of the three you might be tempted to hang on the wall. This variegated tripe is cut into large portions and placed in a heavy bottomed cast iron casserole – layer of onions, carrots, parsley, pepper, thyme, garlic, a layer of tripe, a layer of onions, a layer of tripe, a veal's trotter, and covered with white wine. The dish is then lovingly simmered for at least ten hours. You can sing it songs, tell it stories. Entertained tripe will be softer, more unctuous to the palate, more persuasive. The tripe in the window was obviously happy tripe. Not industrial tripe churned out by the cubic yard in knackers' yards, but the tripe of love, hand-crafted tripe, jewellers' tripe.

I have never forgotten this window display. Never has a load of tripe appeared more beautiful. And in moments of stress my mind has often gone back to those delicious innards, as to a kind of paradise lost. Gacé was my ultimate breakdown, my 'trip' – a mere vowel, I note, distinguishes the two.

Gacé is not exactly on the direct route from Paris to Tours and I mapped out a detour via Rouen and Brionne. The town, when I arrived in the early evening, seemed pretty much unchanged. I couldn't remember the name of the hotel but I found one which seemed very much as it might have been twenty years ago, and after dinner I went down into the empty streets. And there it was.

The shop surround had been modernised but not the window display. Two large marble slabs decorated with different-sized earthenware pots of tripe. A moped disappeared into the distance on the main road behind me. The municipal fairy lights spanning the narrow street swayed in the evening breeze. The shop window was intermittently lit by the blue light coming from the TV in the first-floor flat of the house opposite where a Madame Bovary from Gacé was watching the movie on TF1 and dreaming of her Rodolphe. I stood there, moved and unmoving. The same man, or the son of the same man, or the respectful successor of the same man, had spent all those intervening years simmering the same tripe and pouring it into the same jars in this same provincial town. Alain-Fournier in the early years of the century had written a haunting novel about a magical place to which one longs to return called *Le Grand Meaulnes*. This was *Le Grand Meaulnes . . . à la mode de Caen*.

Back in my room at the hotel, before going to sleep, I opened the Michelin maps and dreamed of a book I would write called *La France des pannes* – Breakdown France: a list of all the small towns in France in which it would be a joy to blow a gasket: Cucuron, Buzançais, Campestre-et-Luc, Pierrefiche, Fréjairolles, Busque, Briatexte, Esparsac, Lalanne, St-Créac, Caupenne, Les Dodins, Propsat, Bongheal, Avrillé-les-Ponceaux, St Symphorien de Mahun . . . And I fell asleep. I was, yes, *à* Gacé, but far from *agacé* – annoyed. The permanence of tripe in a changing world was balm to the soul.

The following day I got up late but just in time to buy myself a very large pot of souvenir tripe. I couldn't take this to the Delluc as a present, they might find it an insulting comment, but I couldn't leave without it. I fingered it in the boot, watching the solidified jelly move under the pressure.

I arrived around six o'clock at Pont de Ruan south of Tours in the Vallée de l'Indre. Edith Delluc came out of the mill house to greet me as I was trying to conceal the bright red Mazda discreetly behind the array of black BMWs and Mercedes which were parked on the gravel in front of the stable block. She was wearing riding trousers very tight at the hips, a short jacket, a white shirt with a scarf around her neck.

'Michael! *Quel plaisir!* I am so pleased to see you. I 'ope the journey was not too difficult. *Bison fûté* said that today was a *journée rouge.*'

The fact that Big Chief Cunning Bison had said that today would be a red one didn't mean much too me – I learned later she was referring to the traffic forecast – but I concurred to avoid the *tarte/plouc* syndrome.

'You left at what time?'

'Actually I left yesterday.'

'*Hier?! Vous êtes parti hier?*'

'Yes, er, Edith, I . . . yes . . .'

She looked shocked.

'But Michael! Surely you have not spent two days coming from Paris?'

I said nothing as I sensed she wouldn't understand the tripe pilgrimage.

'It is only 250 kilometres. There is a motorway!'

I had made a blunder. The fact that the French kill each other like flies on the roads is of little importance when compared to the demands of courtesy. When you are invited for *le weekend* it is imperative that you make the journey in record time.

'*Incroyable!* Paris to Tours in thirty-two minutes! *Extraordinaire!*'

All those little old men in tiny Peugeots who overtook me doing 110 miles an hour were clearly driven by this same desire to be polite. The owner of a *résidence secondaire* must never be given the impression that his house is far from Paris.

Roland Delluc, who had joined Edith, gave me a saccharine smile.

'The English, *ma chérie*, do everything slowly . . .'

Did Edith's pleasure in seeing me annoy him?

As we crossed the vast living room smelling of wood smoke and wax polish, Edith took me by the hand in the most natural and friendly of ways.

'You must feel quite at 'ome, Michael!'

Indeed the whole house was decorated in what the French call *le style anglais*. Impossible to move without bumping into a flowery pouffe. Huge parchment-style lampshades decorated with hand-painted roses draped their heavy silk fringes on to a porcelain base of bright peonies. I had left Abesbury to flee this kind of horticultural nightmare but it pursued me to Pont de Ruan. My room gave on to the millstream – *le bief* – useful for sentences like 'Sod! I've dropped my rush hernia belt in the millstream'. Edith plumped the mattress with her two hands and looked at me.

'Too soft?'

Was she trying to tell me something?

'No. Perfect.'

'*Ah . . . les Anglais!* We never know when to believe you!'

Did Edith's badinage conceal a note of annoyance? Was I supposed to be more difficult? Had my Englishness lost its charm? I suddenly felt on edge.

Dinner did nothing to set my mind at rest. Five couples had been invited: a fat aristocrat who reared labradors and her husband who worked in the Paris office of Sotheby's; an affected short-sighted estate agent with a lisp, married to a journalist from the local paper, *La Nouvelle République*; a movie-mad doctor who knew all the dates and all the films – '*Si si, je vous assure!* Julien Carette – the same one as in *La Règle du jeu* – I promise you. In 1947!' – and his interior-decorator wife who maximised her knowledge of minimalism; a banker and Mrs banker; and the ex-world champion of kite-flying and Mrs kite. Plus me. Which made thirteen. This was the second time Roland Delluc had played this trick on me. The movie doctor offered to go into Tours to buy an inflatable doll to keep me company. We all had a good laugh.

It was not easy to remember the names of the guests.

The women all had cheeky nicknames like Bibiche, Nanette, Loulou. The men on the other hand were addressed in far more formal fashion – Bernard-Henri, Henri-Bernard, Paul-François, François-Paul, Arthur-Georges. In the long run I found I could best distinguish them by their eau de toilette – Y, Eau Sauvage, Habit Rouge, Armani – which compensated for their odourless conversation.

During the dinner Roland Delluc did his Balzac turn. Balzac, he told us, preferred the Indre between Pont de Ruan and Saché to the Loire at Tours. And Roland, with the authoritative brio of man who has bored the knickers off his guests for the last century, quoted from *Le Lys dans la vallée*: '*La magnifique coupe d'émeraude au fond de laquelle l'Indre se roule par des mouvements de serpent . . .*' Balzac, in fact, didn't like Tours at all. It was '*La ville la plus triste du monde*'. The guests politely protested but the lecturer pursued. It is true is it not, *n'est-ce pas*, that we all prefer Madame de Mortsauf to César Birotteau? He proposed a visit to Saché tomorrow. A must. A return to the very source of *La Comédie humaine*. We could even visit the places which inspired the dwellings of Frapesle and of Clochegourde. Wow. My monkfish, which was using the rice as a pillow, yawned noisily in its sauce. It was alone in being bored. The guests were enthusiastic: '*Quelle bonne idée!*'

Edith, a twinkle in her eye, promised even more delights.

'*Vous allez voir ce que vous allez voir.*'

The real rave was yet to come.

Exhausted after the thirty-two-minute drive from Paris and lulled into a listless torpor by the Delluc lecture, we all decided to go to bed early. We had to be in tip-top condition for the *réveillon*. We all chose a magazine from the coffee table to read in bed – Flower Arranging, Wooden Speedboats, Bear Hunting in North America. I took a glossy number on tax havens and stopped at the door to wish the assembled company good night.

'*Bonne nuit, m'sieurs dames.*'

And they all fell about.

'*Il est impayable, ton Anglais, Edith.* He is so funny!'

If they find me a hoot, *tant mieux.* But why? My abbreviation, it transpired, was very working-class. Edith found it charming.

In the middle of the night I got up. I had already had enough trouble with a colonel on the roof rack. I wasn't going to go through the same nightmare with the tripe in the boot. I crept downstairs in the sleeping house and hid my booty at the back of the huge American refrigerator in the kitchen. And went back upstairs with the firm intention of sleeping on late the next morning.

Vain hope. At six o'clock there was a military knock at the door.

'Up, Michael. *Debout!* We're off. *On y va!*'

Off where? Obediently I dressed and went downstairs. The men were sitting at the dining table, their hair still glistening from the shower, eating a copious breakfast – rillettes, pâté, brioches, homemade jam. They were all dressed the same – Lacoste sports shirts and American loafers – *des docksides* – without socks, their glasses worn on a thin cord around their neck. I was the only one to drink coffee. They all drank tea which they called 'teeeee' in order to make me feel at home.

'*Je prendrais bien encore du "teeeee", s'il vous plaît, Hugues-François.*'

When Edith came down to join us, looking very beautiful in a black satin Japanese dragon-embroidered dressing gown, they all stood to kiss her hand. What was I to do? It was six-thirty in the morning and I was still warm from my tripe dreams. I could have followed suit. But I have never done a *baise-main* in all my life. No, I tell a lie. I did once when I was playing the Liechtenstein consul in a school play. I had studied the technique. The hand is presented. You take it and give it a gentle forty-five-degree flip towards the right as if you had decided to peek under a pancake. You then stiffen the upper part of the body like Erich von Stroheim in Renoir's *La Grande Illusion* and you bend this stiffened bust at a sixty-degree angle, lowering it rapidly to within a millimetre or two of the hand. At which juncture you stop. No touching, no licking is required. Proximity is the name of the game.

Edith gave me her hand. I took it and shook it. The estate agent looked at me disdainfully. Too bad. Anyway he was so short-sighted I caught him later in the day in the garden giving a *baise-main* to a rhodendron.

Wellington boots and warm jackets were shared out. It was only when I was given a gun that I realised that we weren't off to the source of the *Comédie humaine*. I started to protest but my reticence would have created a very bad impression, and, not wanting to compromise my friendship with my hostess in the satin dressing gown, I shut up. Armed to the teeth in our camouflage jackets we trooped off in the greenish ugly pre-dawn light to the marshy meadows around the lake. The banker was the ring-leader. He gave us our orders. I was told to lie down in a puddle of muddy grass alongside Eau Sauvage and not to move or breathe even to dislodge the thistle between my thighs. I felt ill at ease with my Kalashnikov. Which end did the bullet come out from? I prayed silently that the ducks would twig what was going on, take another route, go by train. In vain. On the dot of 7.30 flocks of ducks started to swarm over the lake. Why the hell do they do it? Surely they should have known. Didn't some old ducks survive to tip the wink to other generations? Beware mills. Beware parked BMWs. Wear flak jackets. Surely they could see the danger from up there. Nothing of the kind.

Et tactactatctatctatctatctatctatctatc!

Which is the noise French machine-guns make.

It started to rain ducks. So as not to draw attention to

myself I fired my gun, aiming at the Paris–Madrid which was passing at some 20,000 metres. The massacre was all over in a very short time. The sky now clear and duckless. Gamekeepers appeared from the woods with their dogs and set about rounding up the booty, throwing the soft lifeless animals into plastic bags. We could have them for lunch. At least ten each. Yummy. *Miam*.

Conversation at lunchtime centred on the local aristocracy. Poor things. They had a very hard time of it. We didn't envy them at all. A castle was a real burden. All those roofs to repair. The Marquis and Madame de Champlain had bought a garage and sold cut-price tyres in the car park of the local hypermarket. The Count and Countess de Beaupré had converted the outhouses of their castle into eighteen *chambres d'hôte*. They were so successful that they were both on the verge of a nervous breakdown. *La particule* – the magic 'de' indicating nobility – was a hard cross to bear.

My lining was beginning to crack.

Siesta. I dreamed of being pursued by ducks with plastic Monoprix bags on their heads.

Five o'clock.

'*Teeeee*, Michael?'

Am I happy? Am I *à l'aise Blaise*? *Non, Monsieur*.

The *réveillon* ordeal began at nine o'clock. The more ill at ease I felt, the more Roland Delluc enjoyed himself. The men awaited the ladies around the open fire, sipping champagne distinguished by its tired, overweight bubbles and its nose of damp pullovers. Roland strikes again. They were elegantly dressed – wearing the velvet smoking jacket their father wore at the Travellers before the war. The women were heavily made-up and lightly dressed. I noticed that they were on the whole much younger than their husbands. I regretted not having worn a dress myself. They would have found me even more English.

The obligation to succeed, the duty to have a good time,

weighed heavily upon the evening. Everyone was tense. They told stories about other people who were always the life and soul of the party – *Ah, sacré Laurent!* – but who were unfortunately not present this evening. The dinner was good but unexceptional. We should have been eating the rare – larks' tongues, peacocks' wings, bats' cheeks – but instead we were confronted with the three hundred and twenty-fifth portion of *foie gras* of our lives. Disappointment was buried under a plethora of adjectives.

'*Sublime.*'

'*Magnifique!*'

'Cooked to perfection. *A la perfection!*'

The conversation, like the ducks, began to fall from the sky.

Hugues-François was the star turn of the evening. How lucky we were to be sharing our boar with a world champion. After a brief sixteen-minute résumé of the history of the evolution of the kite, Hugues-François moved on to what everyone was waiting for: the statistics. Some three hundred thousand kites are sold in France every year. Golly! There is even a national federation of kitistes, kitiers, kitefliers, you name it. The competition kite with its spinnaker delta wing, its carbon and fibreglass structure, bears the same relationship to the traditional kite – with its ash frame and cotton wing – as does the VTT to the traditional bike. *Comme c'est fascinant!* Hugues-François' title was won at the world championship at Le Touquet in 1994. Specially for us, he reconstructs the dramatic moments of the final. The most important thing is to remain relaxed. If you are not in harmony with yourself, the kite will not respond. We listen, pretending to be agog, using the same adjectives as for the *foie gras*.

'*Sublime!*'

'*Magnifique!*'

But deep down we are bored out of our minds. We'd be

more interested if he'd been flying *foie gras* on the beach.
Panic threatens.

Edith must have noticed the expression on my face.

'Michael. You are very quiet. *Quelque chose ne va
pas?*'

Caught on the hop, I spluttered. Everyone turned to look
at me. Roland moved in to attack.

'*Il s'ennuie.* He's bored.'

'Is that true, Michael?'

'Actually, *en effet* . . . well . . .'

Roland put the knife in.

'Would you care to tell us what does interest you, Mr
Sadler?'

Sitting there in silence listening to the finals at Le Touquet
had given me time to soak up a certain quantity of Château
Chocolate Carpet 1956 with which mine host had decided
to regale us. I took the bull by the horns.

'Actually . . . you, Monsieur Delluc.'

'*Moi?!*'

'No. You plural. I mean . . . underneath it all. *En dessous.*
What's going on? That's what I'd like to know.'

Intellectually I was on a sticky wicket.

'Underneath *quoi, Monsieur Sadler?*'

'Underneath the conversation, Monsieur Delluc.'

'I'm not sure that I follow you.'

'Hugues-François for example . . . Is he never tired of running up and down the beach with his carbon thingamebob.'

They all liked the word.

'*Tinga mi bobbe.*'

What fun.

'*Alors, Hugues-François. Tu t'emmerdes avec ton "tingam-
ibobbe"?*'

Hugues-François looked at me with the beginning of
a smile.

'Obviously,' he said.

Thank you, H-F. You're a pal.

'You see what I mean. That's what interests me. When Hugues-François is pissed off with his kite.'

Silence. It must be obvious I've been on the bottle. Suddenly Edith comes to my rescue.

'I understand! I see what Michael is getting at!'

'Do tell,' said her husband, who had abandoned sugar for vinegar.

'He wants to play the truth game.'

It was as if they had all been waiting for it.

'*Le jeu de la vérité. Quelle idée géniale!*' said the fat labrador. 'And to begin with, let me tell you, Monsieur Sadler, dogs fart!'

Everyone laughed. The journalist took the mike.

'And journalists are lying piss artists.'

The estate agent was in seventh heaven. He knocked on the table to attract our attention.

'I have a confession to make!'

And he got on his knees as if on a prie-dieu.

'Spit it out, Georges-Henri!'

'I've been dying to say it for years. For the last God knows how many *réveillons.*'

'Come on . . .'

'I hate *foie gras*!'

'No!'

'Hate it!'

'What would you like to eat then?'

'Chips!'

'*Des frites?!*'

'*Génial!*'

'Who wants chips?'

And the whole party began to bang on the table with their knives and forks, chanting: '*Des frites! Des frites! Des frites!*'

The evening ended with everyone in the kitchen peeling potatoes. The poached bass with fennel was given to the cat, the age-old booze was poured down the sink and replaced with a seventeen-franc Nicolas Côtes-du-Rhône. At 23.30 we opened tins of crème Mont Blanc which we ate from the tin with a spoon. We were drunk, we were happy, we were friends, we were having a good time at last.

'*C'est grand!*'

Edith adored me. I had turned a terrible evening into a great party. I was the unfreezer. She drew me towards her and kissed me on both cheeks. Like a lingering finger under a crumble, each kiss lasted a fraction of a second longer than a thank-you kiss needed to last. Or was this my imagination?

Just before the stroke of midnight, as we prepared to turn the page, we formed a circle in the kitchen, linked arms and I taught everyone the words of '*Ce n'est qu'un revoir*' – 'Auld Lang Syne' – in English. After this we all kissed again – which allowed me to confirm the fractionally protracted duration of Edith's embrace. The men then took off to the garden to ring their first wives on their mobiles.

To sober up we all did a few laps of the gardens in our shirt sleeves and returned to the kitchen for a Viandox – the French equivalent of Bovril – which sent everyone into raptures as the taste carried them back to childhood.

'*Mais c'est proustien le Viandox! Carrément proustien!*'

The party, which had started so badly, had been a huge success. We smugly spared a thought for all those poor sods in Touraine who were at this very moment screwing up their *réveillon* with Romanian *foie gras*, flaccid streamers and false *bonhomie*.

'*Des frites! Des frites!*'

You only had to say it, everyone fell about.

In the middle of the night I came back down the huge wooden creaking staircase on tiptoe and silently opened the kitchen door. The whole room was bathed in full moonlight. In the bottle rack of the American refrigerator I found my Condrieu half empty. Roland must have had a secret slug to remind himself what wine really tasted like. I poured myself a glass and cut a small cold slice of tripe before taking it back upstairs.

Heaven.

16

The following morning as we prepared to leave, we exchanged visiting cards and made *des promesses en l'air* to see each other again.

'We should form a club!'

'The Chip Club!'

'*Les friteurs!*'

'*On a certainement la frite!*' They were certainly all still in high spirits. But I had another idea in mind.

'I refuse to go back to Paris without a dozen farm eggs.'

Everyone approved. In fact they couldn't give a fart about farm eggs. The nearest they ever got to an egg was a boiled one stuffed with caviar chez Bocuse. But to buy some at the farm – what a chic idea!

Where was I going to find them? Roland Delluc, doubtless delighted that I was going, suggested I go and see Saturnin.

In truth I had already spotted Saturnin. The eggs were only a ruse. Saturnin lived in a rundown farm some two or three hundred yards from the Delluc estate. The roof was in bad need of repair, and there was a hole in the tiles to load the grain into the attic. I'd seen Saturnin in the middle of a field. He was . . . contemplating? Pissing? Both at once? I was drawn to his peasant bulk. I later saw him going into the village on his bike with his wife Delphine some ten yards behind him. He pedalled with his knees splayed because he'd rested his gut on the cross bar. Saturnin, I was convinced, must eat the most amazing food.

I had this fixation that in the French countryside I was

going to rediscover authentic tastes – the way food was before it got in the hands of multinationals and hyper-markets, before freezers and vacpacks, before dehydrated chickens and inflatable *blanquettes*. Because, let it be said, democracy, which has been reasonably effective for people, has been a disaster for food. Take the example of smoked salmon. In the local Auchan they sell it by the yard. If you buy too much, you can use the rest to make curtains for the downstairs bathroom.

A peasant – *un vrai paysan* – with a *gitane maïs* stuck to his bottom lip – must be a living museum of how things were. I went to get my eggs.

My arrival in the farmyard, attractively decorated with several wrecked cars, concrete rabbit hutches and a few tonnes of dung, was heralded by the dispatching of a posse of yelping one-eyed dogs. Saturnin, passive, querulous, sus-picious, majestic – in a word, *méfiant* – appeared on the doorstep of the farmhouse and didn't move. It was for me to approach him, as the canine messengers went back and forth to their master telling him bad news about the foreign egg-scrounger. I explained to Saturnin that I had been sent by Roland Delluc. The price of eggs immediately shot up. Without saying anything, he cruised slowly out into the courtyard and started collecting the precious booty under a bale of straw, in the rabbit hutch, in the glove compartment of a broken down orange Renault 12.

To pay for them we went back to the house. I was approaching my goal. Maybe Delphine was cooking – a ragoût, a daube? The kitchen was filthy, two cats were playing on the gas rings of an ex-white, age-old Brandt cooker. Unwashed plates had been piled up in the stone sink and the walls were different shades of brown because of the smoke from the wood fire which seemed intent on using the door as a chimney. On the huge main beam, antlers adorned with Christmas decorations, and on the wall a large framed colour photograph of a cow.

'*Umm. Ça sent bon.*'

In fact it didn't smell good. It smelled like shit but I was on a mission and I wanted to steer the conversation round to cooking. With immense subtlety I added, 'You must eat well!'

It worked. Saturnin took the bait. His beady eye lit up and his fag changed sides, rolling slowly like a log on a Canadian river.

'*Pour manger bien on mange bien pardi!*'

Pardi! a familar interjection derived from Par Dieu.

'If they want to drop it, they can drop it!'

I didn't follow.

'Drop what, Saturnin?'

'*La bombe. La bombe atomique!*'

Saturnin winked, put a finger to his lips, stood and signalled me to follow him. He led me towards the cellar. My plan was working beyond my wildest dreams. He opened a heavy battened wooden door and went into a cool dark room smelling of damp and animals. There, like an incongruous altar in the midst of all the medieval muck, vast, white and modern, was the pride and joy of his heart. The 250-cubic-litre two-year-guaranteed Polish-built freezer. Whisking a large cat off the lid with the back of his hand, Saturnin opened it. True, I had been expecting to see row upon row, shelf upon shelf of lovingly labelled pots of preserves. But even peasants must move with the times. Saturnin beckoned me to approach. Like Merlin the magician in the icy cloud which rose from the depths of the freezer, he smiled his contented smile.

'They can drop it when they want!'

My heart was beating fast. I was a gastronomic archaeologist. I knew I was about to set my eyes upon a frozen treasure, on bygone grub, on a vision of food as it used to be. I looked down into the depths of the trunk. What did I see? Countless stacked packets of McCain's skin-on chunky country-style ready-cut chips; innumerable deep-frozen industrial baguettes from the Leclerc hypermarket; an extraordinary collection of boxes of an ice cream called Princess – macerated in marc de champagne and then poured into miniature *mousseux* bottles made by Miko. Worse, as my eyes became accustomed to the dark, I could make out, stacked ceiling-high around the altar, packs upon packs of long life UHT milk.

This was not what I had come for.

Saturnin was not aware of my disappointment. He was dreaming. They'd learn their lesson the hard way, those smart-arsed Parisians. The atom bomb has just fallen on Pont de Ruan. Saturnin and Delphine watch me crawling around in the radioactive mud of the farmyard.

'*Saturnin! S'il vous plaît!* A deep-frozen industrial baguette! Just one. *Pour l'amour de Dieu!*'

But Saturnin is unmoved. I am paying the price for those years of frivolity spent eyeing up girls in miniskirts while he was milking the cows. Protected from the deadly radiation behind the sellotaped windows of the farm, they lick a Princess and watch me writhe. The television hasn't worked since the apocalypse. At least dying Parisians provide some entertainment.

Saturnin offered me a drink. Delphine knocked a duck from the table, took the mustard glasses from a three-legged buffet and passed a dirty bottle to Saturnin. He uncorked it, sniffed approvingly and poured a colourless liquid into each glass.

'*A vot' santé!*'

'Your health, Monsieur Saturnin, Madame Delphine.'

And we chinked glasses. And I drank.

The effect was immediate. An atomic bomb had fallen in my gut. I had immediate third-degree burns to the throat and the intestines. I was also blinded and temporarily deaf. Saturnin was delighted. He was having a great morning. Nothing like selling eggs!

'*Elle est bonne, la gnôle.*'

So that's what it was. *La gnôle*. I couldn't ask because my voice box had been destroyed. What a wonderful word. *Gnôle*. This is what I had come for. I forgot the freezer. This was the taste I had been looking for. Here it was, the primeval, atavistic, ancestral, primitive, savage mouthful I had longed to ruin my health on. *La gnôle*. The white spirit made from what's left over after the grapes have been pressed. The very name welled up from the depths of time. Roland must have had a swig of this before the battle of Roncevaux!

'*Elle est bonne!*'

Saturnin dipped his five McCain-style chunky country fingers into the mustard glass, took them out and, with his lighter, lit each one like a match. And, as if the divine spirit had descended upon the apostles, small blue flames lit the head of each Pentecostal finger.

17

The seventh of January. After Christmas and the New Year the pecker of the *Club des cinq* is at half-mast. Until then all had been expectation and salivation. The big meals are now things of the past. On the first of January you enter the vale of attrition. 'There comes a time when you have to pay the price,' said Gilberte. *Il faut passer à la caisse.*

We met – *tradition oblige* – chez l'Asperge. Doubtless all apprehensive, deep down we hid our concerns under the new Club tie, designed by a cousin of Francis who worked in the rag trade – crossed silver knives and forks on a *boudin* black background. Gilberte greeted us with a premonitory salvo.

'*Ah! Messieurs!* The Day of Judgement is nigh.'

Nothing was said and nothing was served.

We left at 9.20 on empty stomachs for our 9.30 rendez-vous. Goujon, Jean-Claude and Francis were carrying their handbags on a strap around their wrists. Dédé l'Asperge, as befits his rank, had a minister's briefcase. We crossed the Boulevard Montparnasse leaving the security of the 6th and entering the 15th. The door of the Dechaume laboratory was opened by a white-coated receptionist.

'*Bonjour, messieurs. C'est pour une prise de sang?*'

We had, yes, come for the annual, post-festive blood test.

We were invited to take our places in the waiting room where other victims, like ourselves, pale, bloated and resigned, were absentmindedly thumbing copies of *Femme actuelle*. Every four minutes or so a pretty nurse would come into the room and select her prey. My turn came. Elastic around the upper arm, syringe, cotton wool, elastoplast and it was done. Dracula would have been impressed by the turnover. The results would be ready at four. We had seven hours of liberty before the verdict fell.

Back at the Balto Gilberte served us *grands crèmes* and *croissants au beurre*. Jean-Claude announced the plan of action. There was no time to lose. He was going to cook us the one illegal dish in the French cookbook, the one dish that restaurants are not allowed to serve, so great is the health hazard, the one dish wanted dead or alive in police stations throughout the country. We waited with bated breath. He was going to cook the dreaded *raie au beurre noir*.

The Club were in seventh heaven. I had no idea what black butter skate was or meant. Jean-Claude proceeded to enlighten us.

The recipe begins innocently enough. Take some fresh skate – about a wing per person – and carefully remove the outer layer which is nothing but cartilage. Poach the fish gently for five minutes in simmering water and then dry it on a clean cloth. Remove the dark and the light skin. A quarter of an hour before serving put the fish into a *sauteuse* – a shallow wide heavy-bottomed pan – and pour on the *court bouillon*. Leave to simmer for ten minutes. So far, nothing illegal . . . Now, however, comes the preparation of the deadly butter sauce. If by any chance the Badoit citron at the *zinc* is a spy from the Ministry of Health we'll end up in the Bastille. Jean-Claude lowers his voice.

'You put a large amount of butter in a frying pan. You melt the butter on a low flame and you allow it to colour. The fatty matter will undergo three stages of decomposition. The first: the *noisette* stage, when the butter turns a pleasant hazelnut colour. The second stage: *l'acajou* – the butter takes on a mahogany hue. And then' – we lean forward to catch his every word – 'the third and last stage, when decomposition gives way to decadence: the black terminal phase, *le beurre noir*. It is for us to choose. No one should be forced to take such risks.'

Unanimously we go for black.

The final moments of the recipe are divine. You slip into an oilskin, thigh boots and souwester and pour the vinegar into the *sauteuse*. The resultant projections of boiling liquid are worthy of the siege of a medieval castle. When the turmoil has subsided you pour the liquid on to the *raie*, serve with fresh parsley and die young.

Jean-Claude was born in Dieppe. His mother worked in an ironmonger's. *La raie* was a luxury. They were poor but she loved her son. When he came home from school he knew it was skate day because his mother was wearing her special clothes. But even so, the vinegar moment was too much. The *beurre noir* impregnated the whole house. It was everywhere, on the wallpaper, on the stairs, in the beds. After each skate the lace curtains had to be deobfuscated hole by hole with a knitting needle.

Jean-Claude, beneath his rough gruff exterior, had a heart. He loved his mum, he loved his skate. I would have been moved if he could have spoken of me in the warm terms he reserved for the fish. But this was no time for instrospection. The die was cast. This was our last stand before the sentence of the serum. In an hour's time our arteries will be in the same condition as his mother's lace curtains.

We collected the fish from the *poissonnerie* Didier – five glistening kilos of skate packed in ice in a white polystyrene box. Once installed chez Nicolas, we took off our jackets and rolled up our sleeves. We looked as if we belonged to a secret society – each of us with a little cotton-wool ball stuck to his upper arm. Lucien's ball fell into the salad dressing. He fished it out and offered to start again but we refused. We are all blood brothers.

The vinegar moment was extremely dramatic. The Club gathered around the rim of the *sauteuse*, Jean-Claude heated the butter, it turned hazel, mahogany, then ebony, he poured in the vinegar, and we were all covered in the spray from the pan, bedaubed, knighted, blessed by the volcanic black buttery ejections. It was a moment of deep communion.

We ate in silence, so rare, so succulent, so luscious was the dish. The resilient flesh of the skate marrying with the soft illicit undertow of the sauce. We would talk about it later. During the week we would wink at each other at the *zinc*. This was the ultimate *partouze*, a gastronomic gang-bang. Later in life, around the fire, as the reflection of the embers glows in the horse brass, my grandchildren will demand the story.

The dish went round three times. There was nothing left. Jean-Claude rose. He was large. He was crimson.

'*Messieurs. Un toast.*'

We rose solemnly to join him.

'*A l'excès!* To excess!'

We were back at the lab on the dot of 16.30. Full, flushed, serene. Each member of the Club was given his little envelope and his social security sheet. No one opened their envelope. We returned in silence chez l'Asperge. Gilberte served five *fine champagne* and, using the paper knife Dédé employed to cut his tablecloths to size, we unsealed our fate.

The results were extraordinary. France had never known such a performance. Our urea, our cholesterol, our triglycerides, reached untold heights. New Olympic records had been set. We were the champions. Dédé's colleague from across the road rang to congratulate.

Deep down I was rather alarmed. My latent hypochondria must have shown on my face. The veterans consoled me. Lucien perused my sheet.

'Cholesterol: 2.8. But that's nothing, Michael! *Rien!* How the hell do you expect butchers to survive with people like you walking the streets? Eat more red meat, *mon vieux*!'

Jean-Claude proudly brandished his sheet.

'Cholesterol: 4.7. You can say what you like, *messieurs*. But that is what I call cholesterol.'

We stood and embraced each other. The ordeal was over.

Every year the danger is more pressing, every year the risk more great, and every year the pleasure is more intense.

18

Post-it note on the fridge door: buy sugar, oil, pasta, *saucisson*. At the Bon Marché I went straight to the sugar 'gondola' as they are called in French. But the gondola was empty. Sweet Fanny Adams. That is, apart from pure sugar cane flown in direct from Cuba at 300 francs a kilo. Odd. Off to pasta.

Same story. Curious. All that was left on the shelves was hand-crafted, bow-tie-shaped pasta flavoured with truffles. Something was wrong. I knew immediately there wouldn't be any oil. I was right – apart from the hand-pressed immaculately conceived virgin olive oil produced by a grinning toothless grandmother in a hilltop Tuscan village at 120 francs for a 'fiole'. Where had all the groceries gone?

I left the Bon Marché and walked up the rue de Sèvres, something I rarely do because the middle section, apart from an old-world shoe shop, is very boring, to go to ED, the discount supermarket. If the Bon Marché is Abu Dhabi, ED is East Berlin, up the end of a shabby mall, full of tins of sardines in cardboard boxes and lit by flickering neon tubes. Ah! I thought as much. Here there was sugar . . . but people were buying it as if it was gold dust! An old lady is filling her trolley with the stuff. Why buy so much?

'*Et la crise, Monsieur?*'

Crisis? What crisis?

True, my daily reading of the newspaper focused entirely on a lexical/grammatical analysis of the *forme* of the articles and I omitted to pay any attention to the *fond*. What were they all about? Yesterday, for instance, I had read in *Libération*: '*Tout baignait dans l'huile, mais il a dû y avoir une anguille sous roche et maintenant il y a une couille dans le potage.*' Which appeared to mean: 'At first there was sufficient oil in the frying pan, but there must have been an eel under the rock because it is now apparent that there is a testicle in the soup.' Any reference to a currently tense political situation seems totally absent from this interesting if obscure haiku.

I had better take precautions. I bought twelve tins of *miettes de thon*. I prefer whole tunny fish to crumbed tunny fish as the tin seemed to indicate, but that's all there was to buy. Back at the flat I opened a tin, a bottle of sauvignon and the dictionary and switched on the television for enlightenment. We were in the main courtyard of the official prime minister's residence, the Hôtel (meaning a large impressive town house) de Matignon. The commentator invited us to watch *le ballet des décideurs* – the to-ing and fro-ing of the main political players. There was, in order of appearance, the PS, the PC, the RPR, the RdG, the UDF, the RPF, the CGT, the CFDT, not forgetting FO and the CNPF, which made things as clear as fog. Fortunately they all spoke more or less the same language. Under the pallid light of the TV cameras, they set out their demands for *tractations* – bargaining – *pourparlers* – discussions – and *négociations*. In order to get the country out of the mess in which it found itself – it was to all intents and purposes up to its arse in alligators – what was required, at this, the beginning of a new millennium, was to achieve the impossible – *la quadrature du cercle*, the squaring of the circle.

I went down to the Balto for a *jambon beurre* and lent an ear to the political forum around the tart stand. General opinion seemed to be that all this was the guff which bigwigs – *les grandes huiles* – use to bluff the general public into thinking they're listening to sense. In fact it was wooden-tongue talk – *la langue de bois*; platitude. A *pâté cornichon* seemed to think that the only viable solution was offered by a lady called Arlette.

'*Une pétroleuse!*' said l'Asperge with a grin.

Flummoxed by the possible contribution of a lady garage attendant to the country's plight I had to go back upstairs to identify Arlette (Laguillier: *Lutte ouvrière*, far left) and the noun: a revolutionary (making petrol bombs).

I had, however, other more pressing things on my mind. Edith Delluc, whom I hadn't seen or, let it be said, touched since 'Auld Lang Syne', had invited me to a *vernissage* of an exhibition of pastels of chickens – an artist friend who seemingly captured with extraordinary verve the vivacity of the henhouse. She had, said Edith wittily, a wonderful *patte*. What had I missed? *Patte* means 'claw' as of chickens' hands and feet and 'original style' or 'gift' as of an artist. It took me two days to understand and I could hardly ring back to laugh.

Roland Delluc had left for Cuba. Full stop. Edith gave me a rendezvous *chez elle* on the rue Gounod. Full stop. No conjunctions. No cause and effect. Two unconnected sentences. I was simply eager to see her again.

I am, as noted, extremely punctual. Edith had told me to come at four – and I arrived at the Decaux *abribus* on the Boulevard du Montparnasse at a quarter past three. Waiting for the 92 I first studied the itineraries of the other buses which share the same stop – the 28 (Porte Maillot), the 82 (Hôpital Américain) and the 89 (Bibliothèque de France). I then read the poster for a film to come out next Wednesday, the names of the stars, the name of the production company, the names of the actors in the secondary roles, the guest appearance by, the names of the authors of the screenplay adapted from a novel by, the name of the lighting cameraman, the composer of the music and all the acronyms of the tax evasion set-ups – the *Sofica* – which encourage the French to invest and lose their money in the movies. I must have just missed the last 92 by a few seconds because this one was a hell of a time coming. But that's the way buses run. Like notes in a Boulez score – I had time to compose fanciful images – they come in clusters. Oddly there was no one else in the *abribus*. After sixteen minutes my patience was tried to its limits. I began to fret. I should have left earlier. There was now only thirty minutes to go. My excessive 'cool' was being cruelly punished.

I decided to take the métro. Less enjoyable, with a long change at Saint-Lazare, but, all in all, better than nurturing an ulcer in a bus shelter. I walked less than a hundred yards down the boulevard to Duroc and went down the steps. *Tiens!* The RATP metal portcullis grill was closed. Odd again. What's up? I went back up the steps and into the small florist's shop to buy a compact bunch of *liliacées bulbeuses* – tulips, to you – and also to find out what was up.

'*Cest la grève, Monsieur!*'

I hit my forehead with the inner base of my left hand in a gesture I had often rehearsed in the bathroom, as if to say, 'What a fool! I should have remembered.'

What strike?

I left the florist's and bought *Le Monde* in the kiosk opposite. Civil servants – *la fonction publique* – are on strike. Quite a lot of people are public functionaries in France. Teachers for instance, employed by the state, are civil servants. As are postmen. And electricity workers. And gas workers. And pigeons. And dogs. What the headlines in *Le Monde* were trying to tell was that it was going to be slightly more difficult to get to Edith's place than I had at first thought.

A wind of panic began to stir behind the left lobe of my brain. I ought to ring Edith but I couldn't. There was a huge queue in front of the telephone box and I hadn't got a mobile. I'll ring her from the flat. No, on second thoughts, I won't. If I did she would tell me to stay put, not to come – what's a chicken exhibition, etc. – and I

want to go. I had a quarter of an hour left. I looked
for a taxi.

Hopeless. The Boulevard des Invalides was now one
compact mass of cars. There was only one solution. I
would have to go on foot. I consulted the métro plan.
It didn't look too far – central Paris is far smaller than
London – and I would enjoy the exercise. It was the right
choice. Walking down the boulevard I overtook the cars.
When I arrived in front of the Lycée Victor Duruy I was just
about to ask my way of two pretty *lycéennes* when I tripped
on the foot of a metal anti-riot barrier and fell on my tulips,
dirtying my trouser knee in the process. My determination
was made even greater.

'You hope to go far like that, monsieur?' asked the young
girl with a diamond in her nose.

I explained that I had a rendezvous on the right bank.
They looked at me and my bent tulips with compassion.

'You won't make it, Monsieur. *Impossible.*'

'*Y a les keufs.*'

Les keufs, *les flics*, *les kisdés* – the police – were, it had
to be said, more and more in evidence as I continued
my way down the boulevard towards the Seine. The vast
open Place des Invalides in front of the military palace
housing Napoleon's tomb was, on the other hand, one mass
of protestors. I came across a group of strikers warming
themselves in front of a fire they had improvised in an oil
drum. They were each wearing a bandanna around their
heads – like kamikaze pilots – on which was written one
word in red ink: there was NON, there was AUX, there was
LICENCIEMENTS – STOP / THE / LAY-OFFS. LAY-OFFS
was bald and the bandanna gave him a very rakish look.
The slogan was of course only effective when they were in
the right order. At this moment they were grilling merguez
on top of the brazier and they kept changing places. When
I arrived they looked up and their heads proclaimed AUX
NON LICENCIEMENTS which made about as much sense

as *Libé*. I do, however, have a weakness for merguez and for them this was a clear token of my political allegiance. It's less a sausage, more of a credo. Unfortunately the merguez they offered me was extremely juicy. At the first bite a red-hot ejaculation of bright orange harissa spurted from the sausage and on to my shirt and tulips. NON was most concerned. I had shown sympathy for their cause and they didn't want to alienate a new recruit by spraying him with North African spices. AUX tried to clean me by using the white spirit they had used to start the fire. The intention was generous, the effect appalling. I was just about to bring the conversation round to the famous stain remover K2R when the police charged.

I have had a certain experience of police brutality. At a gymkhana in Abesbury a police horse once trod on my foot. This was nothing compared with the infamous CRS, the Compagnie Républicaine de Sécurité – the riot police. They arrived from the top of the *place* wielding truncheons behind transparent shields and hitting everything in site – people, trees, cars, even, I had the impression in one heated moment, each other. LICENCIEMENTS grabbed me by the arm and forced me to make a run for the shelter of the buildings on the other side of the road. I was loathe to abandon the merguez – one of them was almost ready, deliciously crisp on one side and rather soft on the other, but this was no time for gastronomic dalliance.

The tear gas bit into my ears and throat. I hid under the archway of an impressive building on the edge of the *place* which turned out to be the British Cultural Centre. Laconic Englishmen were commenting on the confrontation as if it were a football match.

'How long they been at it?'

'Since after lunch.'

'They'll stop soon for coffee.'

The Place des Invalides was now completely empty. I caught sight of my saviour LICENCIEMENTS sitting on the grass in the distance nursing his head. There was a red blotch on his bandanna, which now read LI . . . CIEMENTS. He'd lost a syllable in the fight. The whole area seemed to be covered in blood. Horrified, I ventured forward only to discover that what I thought to be haemoglobin was, in fact, the result of a hundred or so armed thugs trampling underfoot a large number of innocent merguez.

Tulips and Dunkirk spirit in hand I proceded to the Pont Alexandre III – one of my favourites, a slightly over-the-top bridge with monumental pillars and vast golden lions. This morning it was curiously empty. Apart from me and a hundred-odd CRS there was no one about. I realised that I must cut a rather curious figure with my bent bunch of tulips and my shirt covered in harissa, but too bad. It was now 16.40. Edith Delluc must be getting worried and the *vernissage* cold.

The CRS were armed to the teeth and were positioned across the bridge to stop any attempt to carry the demonstrations over on to the right bank. They didn't seem particularly pleased to see me. Opting for a naïve, honest approach I told them I was on my way to a chicken exhibition.

Had I known that '*poulet*' is also French slang for 'cop' I would doubtless have lied or at least chosen another less inflammatory kind of poultry. I was taken *manu militari* to an armoured car behind the lines. The superior eyed me with the disdain normally reserved for a putrid *andouillette*.

'*Qu'est-ce qu'il veut, ce con?*'

Choosing to overlook the discourtesy of his opening gambit, I pig-headedly continued to explain my presence and my purpose. There were no buses, the métro was closed, I didn't understand *Libération*, I had a rendezvous with a Madame Delluc – and I waved my now spicy-smelling bouquet in front of his nose, trusting that he would not suspect me of being a *gentleman-cambrioleur* making the most of the present chaos to ply his trade *rive droite*.

At the word rendezvous, his rockfall of a face broke into a charming smile.

'*Un rendez-vous galant?*'

I could see from the look in his eye that *vernissage* is a euphemism in his vocabulary. He was delighted. He stood. Bowed from the hip.

'*Passez, Monsieur. Passez.*'

And he ordered his men to let me through.

'If you come back this way, let us know how it went.'

He winked at me. I obligingly returned the wink, and as I passed through the corridor of CRS who stood aside to let me pass, they all winked back at me from behind their transparent shields.

On the Champs-Elysées gaggles of secretaries were trying to hitch lifts. On the Avenue Franklin-Roosevelt the smart shops – the jewellers, the galleries, the antique merchants – were winding down the heavy metal shutters. The sky was low and grey, it was heavy, the pavements were deserted, the light dull. It was as if we were on the brink of a revolution. From across the river I could hear the heavy thump of Molotov cocktails and the detonations as the police replied with tear-gas canisters. As I passed in front of the annexe of the *préfecture de police* the incessant ballet of cars, their tyres squealing, their sirens whining, added to the end-of-the-world atmosphere.

Things got even worse on the Place de Pérou. Just before leaving England I had bought a pair of Doc Martens – black, straightforward, without the flash yobbo yellow stitching. It was only on arriving home that I realised that I had bought a pair of 45s when my size is 43/44. I had so much to do that I forgot to change them and it was on the Place de Pérou that I remembered.

I arrived at the rue Gounod at five past six, barefoot. I must have looked like a Valentine card which had been fed through a combine harvester. I ran up the stairs four at a time – the lift must also be on strike – and arrived – *enfin!* – on the plush landing of the fourth floor at precisely 18.07. I was two hours and seven minutes late.

Ddddrrrrrriiiiiinnnggggg. As French bells go. Silence. I rang again.

Nothing. No one.

Pas possible. No one in? I was deeply disappointed and, let it be said, angry. Edith Delluc could have foreseen my problems. She could have listened to the news on the television, she could have heard about a massacre of innocent merguez on the Place des Invalides and drawn her conclusions. But no. Nothing of the sort. Madame couldn't wait. The lure of the chickens was too much. Madame has gone off to her *vernissage* without me.

I felt like kicking the big double doors but I stopped, fortunately, when I remembered I was not wearing shoes. She'd not even left a note stuck to the bellpush. She could have written: 'Michael! Had to leave! If ever by some miracle you make it, do come. Missing you.' That would have been balm to the wound. But no. No note. I'm just about to leave when it strikes me. Fool. Aha. I throw myself on the doormat, pick it up and look desperately for the *billet doux* Edith hasn't left under it.

Now a doormat suitable for a huge dark oak double-doored apartment on the rue Gounod is no hairy postage stamp. This doormat was about two metres long and fifty centimetres wide. It was thick, cumbersome and heavy – weighing all of ten to fifteen kilos. Just as I was struggling to pick it up, Madame de Souza came downstairs from the fifth floor where she'd been cleaning. When she saw what she must have thought was a wrestling match between a *rosbif* and a giant hedgehog, she screamed and ran downstairs. Doubtless to call the police.

I had to go fast.

I would have liked to bivouac on the landing to await Edith's return but that was now out of the question. Should

I leave her the flowers as a pitiful reminder of her heartless-ness? No. They stank of spit-roasted lamb and she wouldn't understand.

Once outside I sat on a wooden bench opposite the build-ing and sulked. The curtains of the fourth floor flat remained obstinately closed. Edith showed no signs of coming back early just in case I'd made it. I was frustrated. I wanted to see her. I was angry with myself, with her, with the strike. Night was falling, I was a long way from home and I was tired, my trousers were dirty, my shirt was covered in orange shit and I had a large blister on both ankles.

I was just about to stand and move off when a youngish man, elegantly dressed, in his early thirties, saw me on my bench. He stopped, hesitated and put his hand in his pocket. Not finding any loose change he thought better of it and walked off.

He's right. I don't deserve his charity. Edith stood me up, that's all.

Elle m'a posé un lapin. A rabbit! *Pour des poulets!*

19

Sixteen days into the strike. The tension is palpable. A demonstration of railway workers on the Place de la République ended in violence: a least a dozen wounded on each side.

Yesterday the class war broke out in the *immeuble*.

I came back loaded from the *marché* Raspail: fish in a freezer bag, snout in *vinaigrette* in a tupperware box, a chicken in a string bag and three kilos of organic apples with worms to prove it. I was pleased with the worms. I once had a goldfish, I've never had a worm.

Bzzzzzclictac. The heavy iron-and-glass ornate main door opened. Enter Monsieur Bandol with shopping trolley. He stopped, immediately raised his right arm as if to say 'Ave Caesar', placed his right foot on the left wheel of his trolley – the small, original wheels have been replaced with larger ones taken from a rotivator – and declaimed:

> *Le choc avait été très rude. Les tribuns*
> *Et les centurions, raillant les cohortes,*
> *Humaient encore, dans l'air où vibraient leurs voix*
> *   fortes,*
> *La chaleur du carnage et ses âcres parfums.*
> (The battle had been hard: the tribunes
> And the centurions, mocking the troops,
> Could still smell, in the air in which their loud voices
>   resounded,
> The heat of carnage and its bitter scents.)

He didn't have time to pursue with the doubtless endless stanzas to follow (by the neo-classical Parnassian poet José-Maria de Hérédia, he was later to tell me at length when I was unable to avoid him in heavy rain in the Luco) because, as if moved by the poetry, the trolley suddenly rolled forwards causing the Poet to fall flat on his face narrowly missing worms and apples.

'*Désolé*,' he apologised.

Two forgiving worms descended from an apple and helped him to his feet. But concussion wouldn't stop Bandol. He took his Sherlock Holmes briar pipe from his back pocket and gave me a knowing glance, seeking my approbation.

'*Alors, les grèves?*'

'The strikes have been very effective. Montparnasse station completely empty of trains was – yes – very impressive.'

I wasn't very inspired.

'*Vous connaissez la solution, Sadler?*'

No, I didn't know the solution.

'*Le super à vingt-cinq francs! Le super à vingt-cinq balles! Il faut les grands moyens.*'

Putting the price of petrol up to 25 francs a litre was certainly drastic, but I didn't immediately see what it had to do with the strikes and he didn't give me time to crack his logic. He'd already moved on to European affairs.

'*Et le Toniblère? Hein? Le Toniblère. Il ferait quoi?*'

How could I know what he would do if I didn't understand who he was.

'*Et la Tatchère? La Tatchère?*'

Got it. He was talking British prime ministers.

'*Elle aurait fait quoi, la Tatchère?*'

I had no idea what the *dame de fer* would have done to save French railways.

'*Rien.*'

There I agreed with him.

'*Ils sont tous pareils!*'

If they were all the same this would at least have the advantage of making our political debate more straight-forward.

'*La troisième voie? Foutaise!*'

He clearly had no time for New Labour. He started to sing the song of the French Revolutionaries:

> *Ah! Ca ira, ça ira, ça ira,*
> *Les Aristocrates à la lanterne,*
> *Ah! Ca ira, ça ira, ça ira,*
> *Les Aristocrates on les pendra.*

Bzzzzzzzzzzzzzclicktac.

Enter Madame Jouvet, fourth floor right, blond chignon and a Hermès scarf.

'*Bonjour, Monsieur Sadler.*'

'*Bonjour, Madame Jouvet.*'

'*Bonjour, Monsieur.*'

'*Bonjour, Madame.*'

The husband of Madame Jouvet works in a ministry. He was an *énarque*. I found this word, in fact an acronym, very confusing at first. What I believed I had heard was '*il est né narque*'. That he was born . . . '*narque*' – an adjective I didn't understand, which is not surprising as it doesn't exist but which I presumed to mean something like 'sardonic'. *Il avait l'air narque.* That kind of thing. Since, I have cottoned on. Monsieur Jouvet went to the ENA, the Ecole Nationale d'Administration, the top-flight school for civil servants. Hence *énarque*.

Bandol and Jouvet don't get on. The former is *de gauche*, the latter *de droite*. And never the twain shall meet. He turned on his heels.

'*Je vous aide.*'

I protested.

'*Non, monsieur Bandol . . .*'

In vain.

'*L'homme, Monsieur, est là pour aider son prochain.*'

And with this deeply egalitarian principle resounding in the hallway around us he picked up the bucket and mop which the Portuguese cleaning lady Madame Vargas always left in a discreet corner and started to climb the stairs. Bandol found it hard going. The bucket spilled dirty water on to the clean stairs but he pressed on. He then paused, and took a deep breath. I suddenly felt it coming. No, please, Monsieur Bandol, not that, not *Le Cid* when Rodrigue's father complains about old age ... But there was no stopping a Bandol in full flight.

'*O rage, ô désespoir, ô vieillesse ennemie ...*'

Madame Jouvet was in no way impressed by the cultural vivacity of Bandol. Her concerns were more for the here and now.

'*C'est terrible, Monsieur Sadler.*'

Her pale hands nervously toyed with the fringe of her scarf.

'We are living a nightmare. What must the English think of us? The English who are so respectful, so orderly, so civilised. What must the Queen think of us?'

As concerns the fact that the French railway system was temporarily at a standstill and that there was insufficient sugar on the shelves in the Bon Marché, it was my ultimate conviction that the Queen, her family, the corgis and the lackeys at the palace couldn't give a tinker's fart. But Madame Jouvet did not want to listen to reason.

'They will have such a bad image of this poor country ...'

A worm who must have been bored out of his apple suddenly decided to make a suicidal dash for it across the tiled mosaic floor of the entrance. Madame Jouvet saw it, screamed and paraphrased Shakespeare: 'There is something rotten in the state of France ...'

If everyone in the building starts quoting the classics we're never going to get anywhere. Fortunately, following the trail marked out by Bandol with the slop water from

Madame Vargas' bucket, Madame Jouvet ran upstairs to telephone to Monsieur Rossi to send in a team of Corsican exterminators.

The worms, standing on their apples, raised their right fists and began to sing the Internationale.

C'est le délire.

20

And then, just as quickly as it had begun, the strike came to an end. Intransigence gave way to realism. The merguez and the brazier were stored away in the garage to await the next revolution. We could at last get on with other things.

I suspected Edith Delluc of having a taste for the abstruse and the recondite. She had lent me a book while I was staying at Pont de Ruan which she had assured me was *pa-ssion-nant*. The book was by the fashionable philosopher/sociologist Jean Baudrillard. It was called *L'Illusion de la fin, ou, La Grève des événements* ('The Illusion of the End, or, The Strike of Events') and was published by Editions Galilée. On page 159 we read: '*Nos systèmes complexes, métastatiques, virals, voués à la seule dimension exponentielle (que ce soit celle de l'instabilité ou de la stabilité exponentielle), à l'excentricité et à la scissiparité fractale indéfinie ne peuvent prendre fin.*'

This gives, in a literal English translation, the following: 'Our complex, viral, metastatic systems, condemned as they are to be eternally exponential (whether this exponentiality be of the stable or of the unstable kind), condemned to eccentricity and to fractal scissiparity, can never come to an end.'

I have tried all that my distant and obviously inadequate university education can come up with to crack it. I have read it backwards, I have read it upside-down, I have read it after three cognacs, I have taken it to bits with a screwdriver, I have left it to marinate in white wine overnight. In vain.

I can foresee a future conversation with Edith.

'*Bonjour, Edith*, you look troubled . . .'

'*C'est la scissiparité, mon chou.*'

'It must be fractal, Edith.'

'How clever of you to guess, *mon cher* Michael.'

'Exponential, my dear Watson.'

I was as a result not wholly surprised by the call I received from Edith as I was having an apéritif with the Club at the Balto. Dédé answered.

'*Absolument, Madame. Je vous le passe. C'est pour vous, Monsieur Mike.*'

Total silence in the café. You could have heard a gin fizz. A woman! For me? The Club was agog.

'*Michael. C'est Edith.*'

Edith's voice, which I had not heard since the abortive *vernissage*, filled the Balto. Impossible in the present circumstances to unburden myself. Out of the question, under the searching gaze of l'Asperge, to reprimand her for her treachery or to talk of the doormat or of my disappointment. Perhaps she rang me here on purpose? How did she know how to find me?

'*Mais Michael, vous m'avez parlé tant de fois de votre cantine!*'

Cantine – canteen, the 'in' Parisian term for a regular restaurant – was of course her invention. She was so sorry I had missed the chicken show, made no mention of having left me holding the rabbit, and had another idea in mind. Cécile, a childhood friend, was rehearsing a play by Marguerite Duras at Bobigny. Was I interested in the *théâtre d'avant-garde*? As yet I was more acquainted with the statue of Margaret in a wet wig than with her work, but I acquiesced. Edith was very enthusiastic.

'*Personnellement, j'adore Duras. Tellement sensuelle!*'

I had been trying to keep my hand cupped around the phone to muffle Edith's voice but her '*sensuelle*' echoed around the café. The Club were delighted. *Sacré rosbif!*

Worse. I dropped the phone on the floor. Edith's plain-
tive voice was there in front of me lying on the floor of
the Balto.

'Michael! Michael!' Wherefore art thou?

Lucien Goujon picked up the phone with the grace of
a butcher retrieving a slippery kidney. Edith was still on
the line.

'*A demain, alors!*'

'*A demain.*'

Click.

Five pairs of eyes asked one question. Who was she?

'*C'était un ami.*'

Dédé, convinced I was leading a double life, corrected the
gender of my French.

'*Une amie.*'

I saw a way out.

'*Non, un ami.*'

'*Qui s'appelle Edith?*'

I bluffed. He must have misheard.

'*Eddie. Qui s'appelle Eddie.*'

They didn't think Eddie was a very French name. Jean-
Claude suddenly found the solution. He was in seventh
heaven.

'*Je sais . . .*'

'*Dites alors!*'

'*Je comprends tout . . . Eddie! Son copain . . . C'est clair!
C'est un travelo!*'

Jean-Claude fell about. He cried with laughter and slapped
me on the back. Oddly, now that I corresponded to his
preconceived idea of the English – *tous des pédés, des
homos, des travelos*, etc. – he seemed to like me better.

Bobigny, postcode 93000, Départment de la Seine-Saint-
Denis, population 44,079, altitude 45 metres, is a northern
suburb of Paris. To get there I took the métro, changed
at the Gare de l'Est and got off at the end of the line at

Bobigny–Pablo Picasso. The main street from the métro to the theatre was modern and rather characterless with supermarket multi-storey car parks, motorway bridges and high-rise blocks. There is a futurist tram that goes from suburb to suburb and, as I was early, I waited with some kids who were listening to rap on a ghetto-blaster. What language were they were speaking? French? It was probably *le verlan* – the hip slang formed by taking the last syllable of a word and putting it at the beginning. I thought about having a go.

'*Ho! Mon frère!* [this is how they attracted each other's attention] *C'est qui le keum [mec] à la dio-ra [radio]?*'

But they might think I was taking the piss so I said nothing.

The actors were beginning to arrive, standing outside the door of the rehearsal hall – a vast, nondescript hangar which looked more suitable for storing bananas. They kissed each other four times, and then wandered off in tense groups. When Cécile arrived – jeans, long and thin, sunglasses in her red hair – she was not in a good mood. Perhaps she was preparing herself for a difficult scene. More Stanislavsky than peevish. No one dared speak to her but everyone was excessively pleasant to her minute Yorkshire terrier – a furry fag-end of a pet who followed her about everywhere. *Bonjour Lucas* – Lucas! fancy calling a dog Lucas! – *t'es beau Lucas* and similar crap. And the Lucas in question collected this pollen of admiration and took it back to the hive. Half-past two. Still no sign of Edith. The door opened and, with a slight sense of foreboding, I trooped into the banana warehouse for my afternoon of art.

In the cold half-darkness of the Empty Space, Thierry, unshaven, scarf, long Clint Eastwood-style overcoat, a director who has worked with Chéreau and Vitez, announced that the rehearsal will last five hours, that Time, Silence, Frustration, and Impatience being part of the exercise, no one must enter or leave once it has started.

Bang! The metal grill is pulled down behind me and I am once again incarcerated. First by Decaux. Now by Duras.

Five hours did seem to me to be rather a long time.

The play is called *Agathe*. I had bought the text at the cultural megastore FNAC. I first read the whole piece in thirty-six minutes. This is the first time in my life I have ever managed to read a whole French play so fast. I was rather bucked. I read it again and got the time down to twenty-two minutes. With training I reckon I can reduce it to fifteen.

Thierry requested silence. We give him silence.

They picked up the text cold where they had left it hot yesterday:

ELLE
Je l'aime. (I love him.)
Silence. Lui se tient les yeux fermés. Elle, détournée de lui.
(Silence. He keeps his eyes closed. She is not looking at him.)
LUI
Je vais crier. Je crie. (I am going to shout. I shout.)
ELLE
Criez. (Shout.)
Tous les paliers du désir sont là, parlés, dans une douceur égale.
(All the levels of desire are there, present, spoken, each as tender as the other.)
LUI
Je vais mourir. (I am going to die.)
ELLE
Mourez. (Die.)
LUI
Oui. (Yes.)

Bang. Enter Edith.

She had come through the wrong door and arrived centre stage. I thought there would be a scene. Nothing of it. Everyone was delighted to see her and Thierry, forgetting his stern preface, was charming. Could Roland Delluc be their patron? Edith came and sat next to me on a long bench at the back of the hall. She frowned and puckered her mouth in an expression that said, 'I'm so sorry I'm so late, mon chéri.' The 'mon chéri' was doubtless an overtranslation of the puckering.

Thierry took up again. The real difficulty, the real challenge of the text, lies not so much in what is said, not even in what is implied, in the subtext, but in the extraordinary silences between the lines. We were to embark on a voyage of discovery of the significance of these silences. I have to confess that when I read the play I jumped the silences, which probably accounts for my world record. Deep down I would have preferred an exploration of the *paliers du désir* but there was no choosing. The torrid torpor of the durassian silence was beginning to envelope us when I suddenly sensed the imminence of a grave danger.

Over the last months I had been conducting an exploration of my own into the subtleties of the *petites récoltes de chez Nicolas* – a series of regional wines all priced under 19 francs a bottle. The consequence of this research was that a somewhat explosive microclimate had developed in my intestines. Now it is common knowledge that the theatre often engenders an unfortunate coincidence between dramatic silences and nuclear testing in the lower abdomen. You are sitting there, riveted to your red velvet seat in the stalls, as the actress, her hair undone, her features ravaged, crawls along the boards in an expression of mute agony, when suddenly a siren announces the imminence of a deflagration. What is to be done?

The French have the answer. Until recently – in the teeth of international disapproval – they had been carrying out underground nuclear testing in the South Pacific on an atoll called Mururoa. I decided to adopt the Mururoa solution. I would bury the blast, conceal it from the eyes and ears of the world. Different techniques can be employed. You can roll your mac into a tight ball and hold it against the stomach as a muffler. You can do likewise with a pullover or wriggle the muscles of the buttocks in an attempt to retard combustion. Of course, if you've had a chance to study the play in advance, if you've taken the time to study the *didascalies* you can contrive a coincidence between the outburst and the explosion. But my reading of Marguerite had not been of sufficient duration. Anyway, as will be noted in the text, when the character says '*je crie*' he doesn't – which makes things extremely tricky for the sphincter muscles, unused to the niceties of alienation in the contemporary theatre.

The urgent management of my intestinal silo, essential for the programme of seduction upon which I had embarked, more than somewhat impaired my concentration. I was about to lose control at an extremely dramatic moment – Cécile clinging on to a wall and advancing as if she was on the edge of a precipice – when I a felt a bat's tongue licking my ankles. It was Lucas, the furry fag-end! I had a bright idea. I grabbed the dog and pressed him against my stomach. Much better than a pully. But Lucas, who wanted to see the play, or who didn't want to be used as a furry filter, tried to get away and started grumbling. I held him by his wet little snout but he started to wriggle and growl. All of which lent an unusual kennel effect to the *mise en scène*:

LUI
Je vais crie. Je crie.
LUCAS
Gggggrrrrrrr.
ELLE
Criez.
LUCAS
Wooooffffff.

Thierry was not too taken with this version. He turned to us and barked.

'Can't you keep that bloody dog quiet?'

Whereupon Cécile went off the deep end and gave a performance which provided the major theatrical interest of the whole afternoon. While the cast calmed Cécile down and made Lucas some lukewarm Earl Grey tea, Edith decided to slip away. Delighted, I started to leave with her but my teacher sent me back.

'No, Michael. Make the most of your chance! Stay! Enjoy!'

I stayed. And I made the most if it. I left Bobigny that evening at ten o'clock at night in possession of a secret weapon. If ever I am stopped in the street or in the métro late at night by someone whose intentions are none too clear, I will reduce my aggressor to tears, I will make him cry for mercy, by reciting the integrality of the play by Marguerite Duras that I had the opportunity of learning off by heart in the Bobigny banana warehouse.

Who says the theatre doesn't serve a purpose?

21

I was working at my desk one morning when I became aware of a strange sensation. It was as if an interior decorator had been at work overnight in my mouth laying a fitted carpet of inferior quality. Every time I swallowed I had the impression I was ingesting thick curly beige wool.

The digestive cathedral had also been redecorated. The walls had been sprayed with Rentokil but the work has been left unfinished and the team has departed leaving brushes, stepladders, sanding machines, screwdrivers and *pince-monseigneurs* (plural?) on site. This particular sensation, the conviction that you have been seen to by a clumsy interior redecorator, has a name in France. It is called *la crise de foie*.

The English, according to the French, only discover they have a liver when they arrive in Calais. Until then things have been pretty calm. Imagine then the havoc wrought on the British interior landscape by the first wave of gallic precision bombing. All hell is let loose when an oyster falls from the sky. The enzymes are at a loss. What's to be done with this wierd crustacean? They kick it, spray with gunge, try putting it on a wheelbarrow and taking it to the dump. In vain. And while they're scratching their heads, they suddenly get drenched by a shower of acid young sauvignon. The juices give up the ghost. Go on strike. Leave everything to rot on the spot.

In Abesbury, in these circumstances, you might suck a Rennie. In France the solutions are legion. How can you choose which is the best? The only solution; the Bon Marché technique. *Une dégustation*.

I arranged the tasting for Wednesday morning.

Tasting is a precise and delicate science calling for sensitivity, finesse and receptiveness. It also requires that one be in perfect nick. I began the preparation on Tuesday night. I ate a whole tin of Bulgarian *foie gras* from ED bought for 34 francs with a Sauternes-style wine at 24 francs. This was followed by some extremely greasy *saucisses de morteau sous blister* conditioned in Marseilles with a deep-frozen *gratin dauphinois à la crème* washed down with a very heavy bottle of red wine from undisclosed sources, camembert, five cream éclairs, armagnac. I went to bed immediately after eating, slept with my mouth open, snored heavily and woke up at six o'clock in the morning in a cold sweat in tiptop form for the *dégustation*.

I set out a series of clean glasses on a white tablecloth. I then prepared the various concoctions and hid the packaging. France is understandably proud of its gut-rot medicine heritage and, to be serious, this tasting had to be blind. I took care to note the colour, bouquet, legs and texture – which, in this instance, varied from seasick green to vomit grey. I then proceeded with the tasting proper. The following are my notes:

Gaviscon, pronounced flavours of peppermint with an aftertaste of bicarbonate, long in the mouth, excellent with rich lamb and cream dishes; *Hépatoum*, fresh mint, round, a little short, the '99 most agreeable; *Solution Stago*, a surprising bouquet of bananas reminiscent of *beaujolais nouveau*, to be consumed likewise *en primeur*; *Hépax*, more Italianate with its hint of artichoke; and *Oxyboldine* with its pronounced aniseed flavour would be more suitable as an apéritif. Others were better served as a *digestif – Phosphalugel –* tasting of Seville oranges, and *Gelox –* of mirabelle plums. I had a particular weakness for *Schoum*, with its pale gold *robe*, excellent after a dozen or so fat Burgundy snails in garlic butter: drink at 12° – a pure delight.

These notes should enable anyone so inclined to build the beginnings of an interesting and representative cellar. My only problem. I forgot to spit, ended up with a *gueule de bois* and had to take an Alka Seltzer.

Next month: a tasting of the hundred and three French cures for constipation.

'A little corked, wouldn't you say?'

22

The buds are full of sap. On the Seine, the trees of the Vert Galant – always the first to blossom – are already green. The first cotton dresses flutter in the breeze. An asthmatic butterfly gets its breath back on a pile of old movie magazines at a *bouquiniste*. The café terraces are full, the wine once again cool. You open a window on the bus to feel the fresh air. Lovers stretch out on the banks of the river and listen to the djumbis. Spring is back . . . and with it, the France–England rugby match.

Jean-Damien Prince, the publisher who accompanied Edith Delluc to the dinner at the Bastille, invited me to watch this annual *derby* with some English friends, the Bellings, who had a *résidence secondaire* in Normandy.

Jean-Damien is an incurable anglophile. He wears what he considers to be English clothes – corduroy trousers with turn-ups, tweed jackets with a large coloured handkerchief in the top pocket – and carefully does his hair in an English manner, with a curl, *une mèche rebelle*, falling languidly over his eyes. He invariably finishes his English sentences with 'isn't it' – which comes out as 'izeuntitte' – the rest of the sentence being unfortunately incomprehensible. His jams come from Fortnum & Mason, he puts marmalade on anything that moves, adores crumpets which he serves with smoked salmon and is one of the dying breed who still eat steak and kidney pudding. His presence is announced long in advance by waves of Crabtree & Evelyn and after his shower he rolls in pot-pourri from Laura Ashley. He swears by *The Times* which he never reads and spends his life on the Eurostar. London is for him *the* place to be and he has a charming ability to pass over the poverty and the hype. He, who hates *la pluie*, adores 'le rain'. And he finds it extremely amusing to get up at three o'clock in the morning to put another 50 pence piece in the gas radiator of his ludicrously expensive bed and breakfast in Bayswater.

The Bellings, his old friends, are retired schoolteachers. When we arrive Charles is earthing up his leeks. He is wearing a beret, a *bleu de travail* and wooden clogs which he kicks off when we enter the house. The two old friends are delighted to see each other.

''Ow are you izeuntitte, Chaaaarles?'

'*Ça boome, Jean-Damien! Ça boome!*'

I am introduced. I hold out my hand but Belling, who has not touched anyone over the last fifty years apart from boys on the end of a cane, takes me by both shoulders and kisses me heartily four times on each cheek.

Same performance from Mrs Belling who arrives from the market in her *deux chevaux*. Jean-Damien is thirsty after the journey.

'A naisse cupofti, izeuntitte?'

But the Bellings have clearly put tea a long way behind them. Earl Grey has been given the boot and been replaced by an extraordinary collection of regional wines. Charles, more enthusiastic than gender-conscious, shows us round.

'*Tu ne connais pas cette petite quincy? Il est* absolutely fabulous.'

And he very generously begins to uncork a series of bottles most of which are reminiscent of nail-varnish remover.

'*Goute la chardonnay! Un merveille.*'

The Bellings spend spring and summer in France. They have a wonderful time. And their very large collection of photographs is there to prove it. What they adore most are the innumerable local *fêtes* – the Duck Festival, the Pig Festival, the *Boudin* Festival. They are always there, the life and soul of the party, their cheeks pink from the red or red from the pink, their hands clutching large fatty pieces of local pork and smiling red-eyed into the flash. Mrs Belling's favourite is one of Charles wearing a nappy and a bib sitting on the knees of the lady mayoress being fed a baby's bottle of Chinon at the hand-beaten plum (?) festival in Touraine.

Down to business. We haven't come all this way just for a glass or two of acid. We have come for '*la*' match. We move into the salon, the opposite of the Dellucs' mill – decorated like a *Woman's Own* vision of a French farmhouse with a basket ready to knock you out hanging from every beam. Charles switches on the television. The atmosphere at Twickenham is electric. The English sing 'God Save the Queen' at the same time as the French bellow 'La Marseillaise'. The French cockerel invades the pitch. Flags wave. The nations are at daggers drawn. And the match begins.

I am immediately struck by the reactions around me. Jean-Damien despises the French team. He finds them puny and spineless and is full of admiration for what he refers to as the Churchillian determination of the English pack – six brutish hulks, with broken noses and cauliflower ears looking as if they have escaped from a Hammer movie. The Bellings, on the other hand, their enthusiasm stoked by the vast amount of booze they had for tea, scorn the English, composed for them entirely of drug addicts and ex-lovers of feckless royals, and are over the moon in their admiration for the intelligence of the French. At one point Madame Belling took off her shoes, climbed on the settee, lifted her arms in the air and, mistaking rugby for football, chanted: '*Allez les Bleus! Allez les Bleus!*'

It's history on its head.

L'entente cordiale, round two.

23

Love is a question both of passion and of technique. It is also a question of culture. With a Lithuanian, one would be obliged to indulge in Lithuanian preliminaries. With a Laplander, one would oil one's body with whale blubber. With a Bolivian one would doubtlesss accustom oneself to the wearing of a bowler hat, and avoid injury by taking care to deposit the pan pipes on the bedside table.

My friendship with Edith Delluc had in the course of the last months been infected by a certain *libertinage*. First our fingers met under the crumble. The significance of this initial culinary accident – I would now prefer to say incident – was confirmed by the course events took. Chez Lipp, when Edith was angry with me for the first time, she told of her failed marriage. Her first husband had been a dentist, she a speech therapist. Their relationship had been too exclusively buccal. He took to the bottle and now lived on Saint-Barth, which meant he didn't hurt himself when he fell over *le pauvre chou* because of all the sand. Roland Delluc had made his fortune in sugar – he was a man of great refinement – and had lived for many years in Cuba before Castro. He adored his wife. *Ils faisaient chambre à part*. They each had their own bedroom.

These intimacies, these unnecessary but welcome revelations, were corroborated by looks, *affleurements* – a hand on my hand, a hand on my arm, the New Year kiss – and, very recently, the most daring stage in this slow but exciting itinerary, an invitation to the Comédie Française to see a play by Marivaux: *La Seconde surprise de l'amour*. Until now my knowledge of the French classics was limited to what we had done at school. I remember *Le Cid* by Corneille – not, of course, as well as Monsieur Bandol. I had published a cartoon in the school magazine; Rodrigue's father rushes in to the tripe shop where his son is employed to ask him: '*Rodrigue, as-tu du coeur?*' 'Rodrigue, have you any heart?' In Corneille, courage not catfood. Very witty.

Marivaux doesn't belong to the same century as Corneille. Corneille was seventeenth-century – the period when France and French literature sought a reflection of its present problems in the mirror of Greek and Roman literature. It was as if human nature had never changed and man was eternal. The titles of Molière's plays say exactly that – *Le Misanthrope*, *Le Malade imaginaire*, *L'Avare*.

Marivaux was eighteenth-century and far more my cup of tea. Times had changed. Louis XIV was dead and things were in danger of falling apart. It was a period of instability and the titles of Marivaux's plays smack of the transitory nature of things: *Les Fausses confidences*, *La Double inconstance* . . . And *The Second Surprise of Love*.

Was Edith trying to tell me something?

The Comédie Française is magnificent, all red carpets, marble busts, velvet crash barriers and ushers in DJs. I had time to read the posters and the cast list for all the plays in repertory because Edith was late and the second trumpet call to tell us to take our seats had already sounded. As we walked up the grand stairs to the *orchestre* – the stalls are on the first floor – she gave me her arm. The theatre itself is red velvet and gold stucco – the kind of *moulures* I now knew weren't served with *frites* in Belgian restaurants.

The play was, in both senses of the word, wicked. The two main characters, le Chevalier and la Marquise, are both still hot from their first, star-crossed love affairs.

Her husband died after only a few months of marriage, his mistress has been shut away in a convent. They have both, as a result, turned their backs on love. But, from their very first meeting, they are attracted to each other. They pretend they're not, of course – but they can't help liking being together. They go for walks, have a cup of tea, lend each other books. In fact they're good mates and they keep telling each other how much fun it is being matey. *Mon oeil.* At the end of the play – and Marivaux's plots are often the longest journey from 'no' to 'yes' – in Scene 16 of Act III, when le Chevalier finally gets round to confessing his love, the Marquise comments: '*Je ne croyais pas l'amitié si dangereuse.*'

I looked at Edith sitting next to me. She didn't move but, let's face it, she chose the play and this is light years from *Bambi*.

Once again I decided to take the bull by the horns. My education demanded it. After the Etoile, after Lipp, after the grilled pig's ears, inevitably came sex. When I was at school, I used to hate the summer months. The south coast was invaded by an army of French boys, with their tennis rackets, their immaculate lobs, their pastel Lacoste shirts, their ability to kiss, their spotless tans, and their scorn of Savlon. This barbarian horde from the south, these prophylactic Attilas, played havoc with my harem. The hour of revenge had come.

'Edith, I am ringing to invite you to dinner.'

'Dinner, Michael? Are you sure you do not mean lunch?'

'No, Edith. Dinner. I am very busy during the day.'

Scripted.

'But of course, Michael. What a lovely idea. Unfortunately I can't. I am overbooked in the next couple of weeks. *Je suis navrée.*'

Merde.

Doubtless I had gone too far too fast. That's the problem
with horns and bulls. You rush in where angels fear to tread
and bugger up the china shop. Edith has – who knows?
– been consulting Madame de Souza who told her that
I treat women like doormats. Or perhaps she preferred
my Anglo-Saxon incompetence to my new-found Gallic
determination.

The following day. '*Michael. C'est moi.*'

She doesn't identify herself. I chalk up a point.

'I have *un créneau.*'

Which means a crenelle in a fortification, a parking space
or an opening, a free spot. I plumped for number three.

'But for lunch.'

I'll take anything going, baby.

'Are you free for lunch on Wednesday the fourteenth?'

I thumbed through an imaginary Filofax and assured her
that I could probably rearrange things.

I began to prepare myself for the ordeal with some
trepidation. I have never made love to a French woman.
Is it more complicated? Sex has a four-fold agenda. 1:
preliminaries. 2: acceleration. 3: climax. 4: any other business. How long does it last? Light on or light off? Do I
possess sufficient vocabulary? What if I am asked to do
something and get the wrong part of the anatomy?

I decided to consult the charts in my *Petit Larousse
Illustré*. There were four which were particularly perti-
nent: the skeleton, the muscles, the vascular system, and
the nervous system. I was especially interested in the
region situated in the south/south-west area of the charts
and noted down a good deal of vocabulary that could
come in handy: *sacrum, tête et col de fémur, coccyx,
épine sciatique, tubérosité ischiatique, éminence thénar et
éminence hyperthénar, grand fessier, artère hypogastrique*
(which doubtless played an important role in the underground nuclear experiments), *artère iliaque, veine fémorale,
nerf fémoro-cutané* and the *nerf crural*. However impressive

the list, there seemed to me to be some vital organs that didn't figure on it. I nonetheless copied it out on a piece of paper and hid it under the pillow on my side.

'Excuse me, *ma chérie*, but I've got a touch of pins and needles in the crural.'

'*Mon chou*, if possible, don't lean too heavily on the old *éminence hyperthénar*.'

I had invited Edith to the Balzar, on the rue des Ecoles. This choice was not haphazard. Le Balzar, recently bought up by the chain that owns La Coupole, was 'saved' by petitions and marches organised by its regulars. It is now just as before, when it was the haunt of Sartre and Simone de Beauvoir. It has the advantage of being laid-back, intellectual, '*in*' without being '*mode*', and of serving a mean trotter.

On the morning of the lunch I tidied my papers, dusted the lampshades and squirted them with a *parfum d'intérieur* called Seville Nights that I had bought in a smart shop near the *église* Saint-Sulpice. I was a victim of oversquirt and the flat smelled half like a brothel, half like a marmalade factory. I bought a cassette of smoochy South American songs – the kind of music that whispers in your ear dirty words in Portuguese. Slightly feverish I took three showers and splashed water on the wooden *plancher* which I had to mop up. Looking for a hanky I blew my nose on the list under the pillow and had to write it out again. I also mistook Seville Nights for Guerlain and gave myself a nasty burn behind the ears. *Du calme*, Sadler. I arrived at the Balzar at 12.44 – sixteen minutes early.

Two o'clock. Edith hasn't come. Now she never will. Disconsolate, irredeemably deflated, I toy with my trotter. All this preparation for nothing? All that for this? What a let-down. What a cold shower. Next door at the Champollion there is a Robert Bresson retrospective. I go and see *Au Hasard Balthazar*, the tragic story of a donkey, patient, forbearing, exploited, wounded. I knew how he felt.

Am I washed of my desire?

24

Buuuuzzzzcliclac.

Enter Monsieur Jouvet.

The husband of Madame Jouvet *quatrième gauche* is an *énarque*. He has a grey suit, short hair, a white shirt, a black tie and and brown shoes. The adjectives are interchangeable. Today, however, in lieu of the perennial briefcase, Monsieur Jouvet was carrying a large saucepan and a plastic bag containing innumerable packets of frankfurters.

'*Bonjour, Monsieur Sadler.*'

'*Bonjour, Monsieur Jouvet.*'

The distinguished civil servant clearly felt the pressing need to explain the presence of these incongruous accessories. He set about the task immediately, professionally, *ex tempore*, without notes, and without ever easing his grip either on the pan or on the bangers.

His children, I must understand, are, at least for the time being, *dans le public* – which means the opposite of what it means in English – 'public' in English, in respect of schooling, paradoxically meaning 'private', whereas in France *public* means 'state' although, he would admit, the same confusion also reigns in France in a similar domain as regards the epithet *libre* – 'free' – *l'école libre*, 'free school', means in fact a paying school, i.e. 'a public school' and not *une école publique*. We all have our linguistic quirks, *n'est-ce pas, Monsieur Sadler*. All this fast and in a monotone, his head firmly ensconced in his shoulders, his eyes fixing something vague and ill-defined in space as if he were reciting a lesson learned off by heart.

Deep breath.

In order to provide what might be deemed a 'logistical service' to Madame Jouvet in respect of the school fête, he had stepped in at the last minute after a much to be deplored defection and taken responsibility – most willingly I must understand – for what was traditionally an important contribution to both the finances and the success of the fête, to wit, the hotdog stand. However – *et c'est là où le bât blesse* – it was precisely there that the packsaddle wounded – it transpired that 87 per cent of primary schools in Paris *intra muros* were holding their fêtes on the same day, with the result that he found himself in the embarrassing position of not being able to hire a hotdog machine.

I tried to alleviate Monsieur Jouvet's burden by offering to hold the banger bag. In vain. The mind was already in overdrive.

Essentially, three problems had to be resolved. All problems and all solutions in France are divided into three. This intellectual waltz – essentially thesis, anthithesis, synthesis – is an obligatory route.

Primo: the container. If one finds oneself deprived of the professional machine, how is one to contrive a situation in which the dog will become – as the name indeed implies – hot? Answer? In a stewpot (the noun was his). But. And there is always a but. Cooking, *non, je me reprends*, warming – for frankfurters, as we all know, are precooked – *donc*, warming a frankfurter in a stewpot is a dangerous operation. *Pourquoi vous me demandez?* I hadn't but he was going to tell me. Because the simmering of the water at a constant temperature, essential for the harmonious heating of the aforesaid frankfurter, is difficult to maintain. A stewpot is *sui generis* opaque. You can't see into the bulk of a stewpot. You can, yes, I concede, examine fleetingly the surface of the water by lifting the lid, but you cannot maintain a constant surveillance of the liquid mass. Now – *or* – the container on a professional hotdog machine is transparent. This is a by no means negligible advantage. The non-transparency of the heating unit in the case of a stewpot would doubtless be prejudicial to the result desired.

Deuxio: the sausage. A quality frankfurter – *vous me suivez, Monsieur Sadler, une francfort pour ainsi dire noble*, whose sheath (I believe he meant skin) – an outer manifestation of its pedigree – is of a pale and hardly orange (he said 'ardly horange') hue, maintains its shape throughout the heating process. It exerts what might, in other fields of activity, be called self-control. Leave it to simmer – *frémir* – happily for thirty minutes and it will emerge from the ordeal just as frankfurter as it went in. But. The second-class frankfurters traditionally purchased by the *comité des fêtes* at a large downmarket sausage retailer's for obvious, if ultimately questionable, reasons of *rentabilité*, such frankfurters – recognisable because of their far more flashy, vermilion hue – do not have the *savoir-vivre*, or should one say *savoir-frémir*, of their more expensive counterparts. They go wild in the water, explode, let it all hang out and when they are eventually fished out of the stewpot they resemble abandoned fluorescent contraceptives (the content of this last sentence has been slightly modified in the transcription).

Tertio: the spike. We arrive at the crunch. The ideal hot-dog machine consists of two distinct components. The transparent container on the right and the chrome spike on the left. The section of baguette – measuring twenty centimetres, the average *baguette non moulée* measuring some 60 centimetres, each baguette thus providing three sections – once cut, is impaled on the chrome spike. But the function of the spike is not only to provide the hole – the absence of dough – for the eventual introduction of the sausage, the spike also fulfills the purpose of heating the bread. Deprived of this second essential element what are we to do? The handle of a wooden spoon will, yes, enable the *préposé aux saucisses*, in the present case himself – to make a round hole in the segmented *baguette*. But. It will be neither warm nor regular in construction. He has experimented in Madame Jouvet's kitchen. And try, he asked of me with a rhetorical flourish, try introducing an exploded frankfurter into a non-straight hole. Impossible. We are therefore left with one solution. To invest in the upmarket frankfurter and sell at a loss. But even then – and it is true Monsieur Jouvet has deep grey, marshy bags under his eyes – even if we opt for the chic frankfurter, what be the fate of a classically erect sausage in a hole which isn't?

Buzzzzzcliclac.

Enter Monsieur Bandol back from the SNCF chorale, where they sing '*Le temps des cerises*' and other songs from the heydays of 1936 and the *Front populaire*. The presence of Monsieur Jouvet in the hall takes him by surprise and, momentarily at least, seems to impair his Pavlovian quote mechanism. Hoping to have a discussion rather than to listen to a recitation I leap in with the helpful, if unlikely information that we're discussing frankfurters: '*Nous parlions des francforts, Monsieur Bandol.*'

Bandol, still warm from the Popular Front and, mistaking my plural for a singular, and my composite noun for a substantive and adjective, explodes.

'*Le franc fort? Le franc fort!*'

I see the danger. But there is no possibility of intervening to tell him that, no, we were not talking of the strong franc and the economic policies of the French right in the 1980s and early '90s.

'*C'était une politique exécrable! Mais exécrable!*'

And, eager to condemn the exploitation of the masses . . .

L'aurore grelottante en robe rose et verte
S'avançait lentement sur la Seine déserte,
Et le sombre Paris, en se frottant les yeux,
Empoignait ses outils, viellard laborieux.

I turned to share my pleasure with Monsieur Jouvet, but *énarque*, stewpot and sausage had already disappeared. Dutifully, I stayed to listen.

I am decidedly too English. Jouvet has the intelligence, I the education.

25

I hesitated a long time.

A love scene has no place in a documentary. The genre is not suited to it. The intimate belongs to the private journal, or to the more confessional strain of poetry and of personal fiction. My modest desire to reveal has, however, strength-ened my resolve to transcend traditional genre distinction and to transgress the rules of good behaviour.

The Balzar lunch – the Balzar balls-up – was, as the French would have it, my Bérézina – Napoleon's terrible defeat on the retreat from Moscow. It was my nadir. Fortunately, the following day, I received the call I had been expecting the day before. I threw myself on the phone like a drowning man on a rubber tyre.

'*Allô*.'

On the other end of the phone a voice whispered.

'Michael. I am so sorry for Tuesday.'

'It was Wednesday.'

Edith paid no attention.

'You were so cross?'

Why all the 'so's?

'Not cross, no. Disappointed.'

A noble quibble in the circumstances.

'Roland had a crisis.'

What the hell's a crisis?

'*Une crise*. An attack.'

Red Indians? *Bison fûté*?

'*S'il vous plaît, Michael. S'il vous plaît. Ne m'en voulez pas.* Do not bear a grudge.'

She decided to talk in subtitles.

'*Venez chez moi demain matin.* Please. Come to my place tomorrow morning.'

The French tell the joke of the Belgian co-driver examining the winking light. 'It works. It doesn't work. It works. It doesn't work.' I am as thick as a French Belgian and as vacillating as his winker. You can turn me off, you can turn me on.

I slept very badly, my arm under the pillow, my hand clenched on the list.

Buuuzzzzzz.

A distant hoover was switched off and purred into silence. The door was opened by Madame de Souza wearing a white apron over her crow-black dress. She seemed not to recognise me without my orange shirt and doormat.

'*Madame est dans sa chambre.*'

Her bedroom!

'*Je vous annonce.*'

Announce me o dark Iberian.

'*Suivez-moi, je vous prie.*'

I followed her through the silent apartment whose opulence seemed somehow less oppressive in the fresh morning light. Monsieur Rossi and the two hoods in Y-fronts gave me a wink of encouragement as I passed through.

'*Michael! Quel plaisir!* Come in! We'll talk English.'

All this explanation I presume for the sake of Madame de Souza, who didn't seem to demand one. Edith was in bed, a breakfast tray virtually untouched on the ground beside her, *Le Figaro* unopened on the plush covers.

'You were so fast!'

Not what her husband thought. And where is he? I looked around me. The scene was almost too perfect. Could this be a trap? Was Roland a voyeur, in amongst the suits with his

Pentax? Was Valmont to play a role in a Feydeau farce? But the doubt didn't last.

'*Venez vous asseoir.*'

I sat on the bed. The weight of my body moved hers.

'*Non. Plus près. Pas trop.*'

The geometry of sensuality is an art.

'*Vous m'écrasez . . .*'

Is that an invitation?

'*Parfait. Ne bougez pas.*'

Pity.

She moved her body a graceful quarter-turn and, with a fine, slender, muscular arm fashioned by years of luxury tennis, she took the internal phone.

'Madame de Souza . . . Do the kitchen now.'

Good idea. The kitchen. Several miles back down that old corridor. The hoover was once again switched off with an asthmatic wheeze which once again reminded me of Delluc. I must get him out of my mind.

'*Alors, Michael. Racontez.*'

She patted the bed. I was required to perform. To entertain. To tell. To tell what? That I had burnt my neck on *Nuits de Séville* and picked up a lot of sexy words in the Larousse?

'I was very hurt when you didn't turn up at the Balzar.'

'Hurt' I judged was not bad. It upped the level of the emotional debate.

'*Mais* Michael! You didn't believe me? You must believe me. Come!'

She threw off the bed covers and slipped her feet into extremely high-heeled bedroom mules. She was wearing a light-grey satin peignoir tied at the waist by a loose satin belt.

'Come!'

I took her hand and we walked back through the vast, empty flat. In a large reception room off the main dining room Edith went over to a stout mahogany chest, all inlaid brass and marquetry, and slid open a drawer. She took out several enormous beige envelopes and emptied their contents over the floor.

'Sit.'

We sat down on the floor in a field of slippery X-ray photographs.

'Look.'

She took one and held it up to the light coming from the window on our left.

'Do you believe me now?'

I didn't understand what she was showing me.

'*Mais son pontage, idiot!*'

His *pontage*. *Pont*? Bridge? The *pontage* over the River Kwai?

'His by-pass! *Ce que vous êtes charmant.* I'll explain.'

She sat me down on the canapé and started to unbutton my shirt.

'Edith!'

'This is a biology lesson, Michael. You have to know all about *pontages* . . . *Laissez-moi faire.*'

Edith was blowing hot and cold at once, calling me *vous* as she slipped my shirt off. The lesson, however, called for the removal of more than shirts. And there, marooned in a Sargasso sea of X-rays, in a room echoing with the memories of *mondanités*, she took all my clothes off.

'We clear the decks, Michael. It is necessary in order to understand. Arteries are very complicated. There is for instance one that begins . . . there . . .'

She touched me lightly with her finger.

'Here?'

'And finishes . . . there.'

And she moved her finger along the route.

'No! That far?'

At this rate I'm going to need a *pontage* myself. I trust she is not going to ask any questions. I've left my list in my trousers and am liable to take my elbow for my *hypothénar*.

'So, Michael. Now, you understand and you believe . . .'

I believed her. I am now naked on the *canapé* from which, one evening last autumn, I had witnessed, fascinated, Roland Delluc make the bet which at this very moment he is in very real danger of winning.

'*Vous êtes beau, Michael.*'

There is a play by Giraudoux in which a young girl gets all she wants by saying precisely and only that to all the men she meets. But I have no time to be suspicious. Edith kisses me. Her lips touch, brush, leave mine. Odd. She kisses me as if I wasn't naked. Her kiss is long but chaste, like a tall nun.

'*Suivez-moi.*'

Edith enjoys to-ing and fro-ing. As we cross the dining room she stops to eat a grape. I am taken by a fleeting moment of panic. What if the door were to open? What if Roland Delluc were to enter to find a British nudist nibbling his bunches. No door opens. We are once again in the bedroom which is hung with heavy Turkish tapestries.

'Odd, Michael. You are not built exactly like a Frenchman.'

Sod. I was sure there was something missing.

'There, for instance, often there is a hollow. *Un creux. Mais non. Pas de creux.*'

True, I was *creux*-less – although I was relieved because the absence of something absent shouldn't excessively endanger the present enterprise.

Edith undid the satin belt and let the peignoir slip to the ground in a sensuous swish. She stood there naked in front of me, slight, firm, proud, her skin gleaming in the dappled light from the diaphanous curtains at the window. She was still wearing her necklace and her shoes.

La très chère était nue et connaissant mon coeur
N'avait gardé que ses bijoux sonores.

Me and Baudelaire are brothers.

'*Venez*, Michael.'

She took me by the hand and stretched out on the bed.

I would at this juncture like to interrupt the narrative momentarily in order to point out, with some insistence, that it is not the object of the following to be in any way voyeuristic or pornographic. What ensues is nothing more than an encounter between two cultures. The transcription is as faithful as possible but I cannot guarantee its total veracity as I was not in a position to take notes.

'Come.'

She slips very lightly on to me. A cloud must have crossed my face. She is sensitive to my atmospherics.

'*Qu'est-ce qui ne va pas, Michael?*'

'Nothing, Edith. Only . . . this is the first time I've made love to a French woman, and there is something I must explain . . .'

'There is something you want, Michael?'

'No, not so much want, as it were, as not want . . . I don't want . . . if you see what I mean . . . to bring the proceedings to too abrupt a conclusion . . .'

'I thought the English did everything slowly!'

I looked at her body, her eyes, her strong shoulders, *la chute de ses reins*.

'You are so desirable, Edith.'

'*Attention*, Michael.'

Quick. Only one thing for it. I close my eyes and recite the multiplication tables off by heart. *Ouf*, as the French have it. Phew! Our honour is saved. The danger passes. England breathes again.

'You see what I mean, Edith.'

Edith laughs.

'But this is fun! We must do something. You are to listen to me. *Bon. Revenez. Doucement. Voilà. Très bien*. And now Michael. Pay attention. You must concentrate. In order to occupy your mind, you are going to explain to me something very mysterious.'

'Yes, Edith?'

'You are going to explain to me the rules of cricket.'

'Cricket?!'

The very word 'cricket' has an immediate effect. She is alarmed.

'You don't like cricket?'

'Yes . . . er . . . my apologies, Edith . . . I was just thinking, the first Test starts—'

'Michael. You must think of me at the same time.'

'You'll find me ridiculous, Edith!'

'*Au contraire.*'

I can hardly see Casanova incorporating this in the catechism of foreplay, but too bad.

'Cricket lasts a long time, *non?*'

'Often five days.'

'*Cinq jours?* Perfect.'

Five days? Gulp.

'*Commencez.*'

'Well . . . Cricket is . . .'

'*En français.*'

'*Au cricket il y a deux équipes . . .*'

'It is so much better when you are two . . .'

'Edith. If you continue to make remarks of a suggestive nature you will defeat the purpose of the exercise.'

'*Pardon, Michael. Recommencez, je vous prie . . .*'

If I'm not mistaken, Edith is warming to the game. Excellent. And it's always opening the batting which is the most difficult.

'*L'objectif de la première équipe est de marquer des* – how do you say it? . . . Runs . . .'

'Mmm, runs . . .'

'*Le jeu commence lorsque le premier joueur entre*—'

'*Comment vous le dites en anglais?*'

'When he comes in.'

'Come in, come in . . .'

Four and half minutes. Not bad. Good heavens. What's happening. We're turning round. Must be the end of the over. For the first time I am in a position to appreciate the wallpaper. An impressive attic panorama of Troy in flames three nines are twenty-seven four nines are thirty-six . . .

'What then, Michael?'

'*Le but de ce joueur est de rester* in . . .'

'*Oh oui* . . .'

'*Et ne pas être* out . . .'

'*Pas* out, Michael. In!'

And five nines are forty-five. Suddenly, by means of an acrobatic movement, we find ourselves both on the floor. There are books under the bed. Edith is reading a biography of Omar Sharif. I wonder what Omar would have to say if he saw me now . . .

'Michael!'

Concentration, Sadler.

'*La deuxième équipe se place dans des positions différentes* . . .'

'What different positions? Show me!'

We are at present upright, Edith entwined around me in a position which is threatening the equanimity of my *tubérosité ischiatique*.

'*Il y a le* gully . . .'

'*Faites moi le* gully.'

Edith is becoming more insistent.

'Faster, Michael. *Plus vite. Encore des positions* . . .'

Tiens! She's losing her English.

'Silly mid-on, silly mid-off, first slip, second slip, third slip, point . . .'

We have reached the door of the bedroom. This is an unusual way to view a flat but I've always been of a curious nature. I hadn't noticed an extremely attractive Louis XIV *bergère* or could it be six times nine are fifty-four Louis the XVI.

'More cricket, Michael!'

'*Et quand celui qui jette la balle détruit le wicket de son adversaire il crie,* "How's that?"'

'Mais c'est bon . . .'

We are now crossing the salon. Edith's questions are more and more urgent, her breathing more and more staccato.

'How does it end, Michael? *Racontez la fin!*'

'*Le bowler lance la balle . . .*'

'*Très fort, très vite . . . oui . . . oui . . .*'

'*Le batsman donne un grand coup . . .*'

'*Un grand coup oui . . . oui . . .*'

'*Ça monte dans l'air . . .*'

'*Ça monte . . .*'

'*Très haut . . .*'

'*Très loin . . .*'

'Will he catch it in time?'

'*Il va l'attraper, il va l'attraper.*'

'*Il court.*'

'*Vite, vite!*'

'*Il arrive.*'

'*Plus vite!*'

'*Ça descend . . .*'

'*Pas encore, Michael. Sur la table!*'

'I beg your pardon?'

With dexterity I lay the table.

'*Vite, vite!*'

'*La balle descend . . .*'

'He is underneath . . .'

'*Il tend les mains, il va le prendre, il prend . . .*'

'*Prenez-la! Prenez-la.*'

And then, sublime.

'*Crickettez-moi!*'

A phonetic transcription of the ensuing exchange, which, it is true, could hardly be described as dialogue, is beyond my linguistic capabilities. Edith cried out. Her body was a bow, taut, stretched. The arrow flew, unleashed. The chandelier shivered, incandescent. Her hand grazed a baroque crystal bowl of Venetian glass fruit. Two small apples spilled from the bowl, rolled on to the table, rolled to the edge, knocked, stopped.

Silence at The Oval.

'I didn't know that cricket could be so exciting, Michael.'

She gently stroked my hair, my shoulders. I looked at my watch. Her eyes darkened, angry.

'*Mais Michael! Tu es pressé?! Tu as un rendez-vous?*'

'No, Edith. But we only have seven minutes in which to be friends.'

She smiled. So did I.

She had called me '*tu*'.

26

I sat in the Café Marly opposite the Pyramide du Louvre. Outside, the water lapped against the invisible edges of the dark marble pools. The terrace stretches along the Richelieu gallery of the Louvre giving on to the Cours Napoléon. Inside, glass walls separate you from the sculptures of the museum. You sink into a velveteen armchair, and lose yourself in the Second Empire splendour. The Café Marly is about as smart as you can get, which was suitable because that was just about how I was feeling. I'd made love for twenty-three minutes non-stop and visited a flat at the same time. I merited my *religieuse*.

Back in the 6th this mood of sex recollected in tranquillity took a bit of knocking. I was walking down the rue de l'Abbé Grégoire when Lucien Goujon leapt out of the *boucherie*, grabbed me by the shoulder as if he was investigating my cutlet capacity, and announced the Big News.

'*Très bonne nouvelle à t'annoncer! Tu vas être content! Jean-Claude t'invite!*'

Jean-Claude invites me to what? To go and take a running jump? To go and cook myself an egg – its French equivalent? Not at all.

'*A son anniversaire, mon vieux!*'

Up until now Jean-Claude had not liked me. His politics were not my politics, my language was not his. And now, change of heart. He has invited me to his birthday party. I was taken with that sudden and rather cloying feeling of tenderness you always feel towards someone who didn't

like you and suddenly does. Lucien couldn't resist letting
me into the secret of the menu. He beckoned me to follow
him into the huge fridge at the back of the shop – *la
chambre froide*. As we progressed down it, our shoulders
nudged haunches, shoulders and gigots all reserved for the
jet set. To each piece of meat on its hook was pinned a
famous name. It was like walking into the morgue the day
after a serial killer had wreaked havoc at a Hollywood
cocktail party.

At the back of the fridge, hidden under a large white
linen cloth, was the treasure trove. He unveiled the dish
and put his forefinger on his thumb in a gesture to express
delicacy.

'*Très très rare.*'

I was sure he was right – as I had never seen it or them
or whoever it was before. The matter on the dish was
pinkish-white, cumbersome, jellifluous if the word exists,
certainly difficult to pick up, which I had no desire to do,
and not exactly mouth-watering.

'*Miam.*' Yum, I lied, all the while pleased with the conti-
nental onomatopoeia. Our friendship allowed me to confess
my ignorance.

'*Mais . . . c'est quoi exactement?*'

'*Ça, monsieur Mike, ça . . . Ce sont quatre kilos de
rognons blancs.*'

Four kilos of testicles! *Ciel!*

In the dish before me there was sufficient ruminative
masculinity to fertilise the county of Hereford. As an after-
math to a morning of love, I could have hoped for a more
tender awakening. Nonetheless, grateful for the honour I
was being done, the next day I arrived at the appointed
hour at the Balto.

As Dédé l'Asperge knocked up the traditional Alexandra,
Jean-Claude and I embraced, both obviously moved by our
new-found acceptance of each other. I had found him a
present, a coffee-table *Histoire du boudin* with a crepuscular

photograph on the cover which made even black pudding
look romantic. We then all proceeded down the rue du
Cherche-Midi to Nicolas where a cool Meursault awaited
us as *une mise en bouche*.

Jean-Claude was fifty-two but you would think he was
at least ten years older. Didier imitated him, hitching up
imaginary trousers over an imaginary gut. Dédé said he's
missed his vocation. He shouldn't have been a fishmonger;
he ought to have been an actor – he could have played in
Le Mérou malgré lui or *La Barbue de Séville*.

Lucien was meanwhile hard at work, crouched over the
slab on which he lovingly laid out the 'white kidneys'.
They were first sliced into thin escalopes with an extremely
sharp knife and then dipped in milk before being fried in
butter and garlic. Lucien had another surprise for us. This
was to be a lunch 'of the extremities'. Before serving the
undercarriage, as he put it, he presented us with a dish of
the most extraordinary-looking delicacy.

'*Une salade de crêtes de coq!*'

Coxcombs! The thought of eating a cockerel's punk hairdo
would have made me sick a few months ago. Now I tucked in
with pleasure. I'm ashamed to say that there are now very
few parts of the animal that I haven't eaten. Toes? Eyebrows?
Lucien has promised me an udder.

The *plat de résistance* arrived. Each member of the clan
ritually covered his head with a large white linen *serviette*
and shut himself away with his testicles. From a distance we
must have looked and sounded like a load of shortsighted
sheiks eating soup. The dish was delicate, appallingly delicious. The silence of the backroom was filled with the
contented sighs – glloup, schlurpp and shrocck – of the
officiants. But suddenly an unwarranted sound interrupted
the litany.

Schloupppffff.

Something odd had happened.

Schlurpp OK. But schloupppffff?

Like scouts emerging from their tents after a night of debauchery, the sybarites quit the anonymity of their *serviettes* to glance around the encampment.

Jean-Claude was lying face down in his *rognons*. We thought for a moment that he was having us on. That this was a joke. That he was pretending to faint with pleasure, but he was curiously inert – and the weight of his head falling into the sauce had splashed Francis's trousers.

As I contemplated my new-found friend immobile in his lunch, I had a fleeting vision of the fragility of all things. Jean-Claude, the son of Mrs Xerox of Dieppe, she who slipped into something special every time she was going to paste the net curtains with *beurre noir*, our companion in arms was lying there before us, his cheek pressed lovingly against a bull's pride and joy, his Club tie dangling in the void, hovering between life and death.

Francis rang the SAMU and the emergency medical service, complete with doctor and firemen, arrived from just down the road and brought Jean-Claude back to life with a shot of oxygen. It was a close shave. The doctor eyed the table with suspicion and asked us what we had been eating. Sheepish and proud, we recited the menu. He frowned.

'*Attention, messieurs! Faites attention.*'

We were all shaken by Jean-Claude's birthday brush. Happiness hangs on a thread. It was Lucien Goujon who restored us to our senses and who dispelled the maudlin atmosphere with a piece of profound philosophy that only a man of his ilk could come up with. It would, he said, have been a wonderful way to go. Just imagine, he said.

'*Partir comme ça . . . La tête dans les couilles. Génial.*'

Food for thought.

27

As soon as the summer months arrive, Didier the fishmonger told me, the Parisians leave for the sea. They breathe in carbon monoxide on the Place de la Concorde for eleven months of the year and go and empty it all out on the beaches of Deauville and Biarritz during the twelfth.

Edith Delluc rang me.

'Michael. *Quel plaisir*. We are leaving for ze Ile de Ré. You don't know ze Ile de Ré? It ees paradise! You must come! Please. Before leaving I 'ave not a moment. But you must come to the seaside.'

'*On va s'amuser?*'

We hadn't spoken to each other since The Oval and she made no reference to it. I was hoping she would – Test matches come in fives, that kind of thing – but no. Perhaps Delluc was in the room behind her juggling with his sugar lumps? I replied that I would be delighted to join them. That I had, yes, once been to the Ile de Ré. But that was a long time ago. That was when you still had to take a ferry. That was a long time before the *pontage*. She laughed and her laugh made me blush with pleasure.

I am doing all I can not to become too attached to Edith Delluc. But I can't help admitting to the fact that I don't want things to come to an end. I jump in the Mazda. Direction La Rochelle. The motorway to Spain is full of happy Arabs driving home for the summer in old Renault 18s with the roof-rack piled high with what looks like nine tonnes of Livarot. From the turning off to the Ile de Ré cars change.

Windows open and Cheb Mami on the A10, Glenn Gould and air conditioning after exit number 32.

The Delluc summer house was an opulent long symmetrical villa with a neat front garden and grey-green shutters giving directly on to the sea. When I arrived early afternoon the maid, who was an insular version of Madame de Souza, was noisily throwing mussel and oyster shells from lunch into a dustbin. She didn't know anything – who I was, whether I was expected, where was my room, who was having a siesta, who had gone fishing and who had gone for a bike ride across the salt flats. True to form Edith hadn't left a note, neither on the table, nor, presumably, under the doormat. The house was silent. I sat on the terrace, read yesterday's *Monde* and nibbled a pizza which carried the same date. From inside the house came the same rich smell of wax polish and luxury I had smelled in the millhouse at Pont de Ruan. Bored, I did a little tour up and down the road on an extremely emasculating racing bike I found in the garage.

Edith came back from the sea around five with a host of beach buddies. She was delighted to see me and delighted to introduce me to her pals.

'*Vous connaissez mon ami anglais Michael?*'

'*Ah, non.*'

'Hello, Michael . . . Haha!'

'How's things haha!'

'Ze sea iz cold izzeunitte.'

They were all very chummy. I was rather put out by the presence of an American they met on the beach and who seemed to have infiltrated the group. I would very much have preferred to be the only foreigner. Gary's presence rendered me less exotic. Worse. He was about seven feet tall, wore a surfboard like a guitar on his back and Bruce Springsteen bandanna in his hair. He smiled all the time and was ready for anything.

'Great! Why not? Great!'

He was also very bad-mannered and a sponger – *un pique-assiette*. You offer him cake, he'll take the cake.

'*Le gatoooooo*, great!'

A cup of tea?

'*Le theeeey?* Great!'

They all found his accent adorable.

The chums start to disperse. I begin to anticipate the moment when I'll find myself alone with Edith. But Gary refuses to disperse. In fact Gary limpets. I am reduced to making conversation.

'*Et Roland?*'

I couldn't give a fart.

'*Ca va, ça va. Il se repose bien.*'

Then we all have to jump back on our Peugeot emasculators to go back into the village of Les Portes to have a drink. Gary in tow.

We take the cycle path. Edith finds Gary hilarious on his *vélauuuuuuu* which is much too small for him. I had been looking forward to meeting people who lived all year on the island – locals, fishermen, farmers. But the fishermen and farmers had either sold up or let their property for the rich summer months. I did spot someone wearing seafaring gear – blue sweater and a Captain Haddock peaked cap – but he turned out to be a Romanian sculptor who had an exhibition at the Met. I had hoped to give Gary the slip in the narrow streets of the village. No go. He stuck to us like superglue.

While Edith was getting ready for the evening and taking Roland out of the fridge, I went down to the beach for a quick dip in the picnic leftovers and elastoplast that the evening tide washed in. When I returned to the house Gary had already laid the table – thereby pre-empting my own au pair number – 'Oh thank you, Michael, you are so sweet' – and by the same token getting himself invited to dinner. The dinner guests turn up – the same pals as this afternoon but fresh from the jet wash.

Necessity being the mother of invention, I did find something to do. I decided to barbecue the oysters. I had never done it before. It takes a great deal of concentration. You put the oyster on the grill, taking great care not to burn your fingers as you keep the oyster upright. You wait a few minutes, it goes pop, the lid comes off and you're in business. Add iced butter which has been flavoured with lime, have a little glass of anything cold and white to hand, have another one, pop goes the oyster, in with the mixture and in no time you're as buttered as the mollusc itself. I was having a real success with my barbecue, until Gary came up to watch what I'm doing.

'Hey, man!'

'*Quoi?*'

I refused to speak to him in English.

'*Arrêtez, man!*'

'*Qu'est-ce qui ne va pas?*'

I tried to make my sentences as complex as possible.

'*Ça, c'est crou-elle! Regarde ce qu'il fait. Avec les oï-stères!*'

The guests gather around my barbecue.

'*Qu'est-ce qui ne va pas? Ce n'est pas "great"?*'

'No, man! *Pas great du toooouuu! Ils sont vivants les oï-stères. C'est crou-elle, man!*'

And the politically correct American proceeds to bore the knickers off us with a lecture on the nervous system of the oyster. Edith comforts me. My oysters are divine. In fact this is the fifth time she has told me the same thing. And each time she gives me a little squeeze of the hand. Has she had a bit too much to drink? Just before we sit down for supper Roland Delluc comes over to me, a sardonic smile on his lips. He squeezes my elbow, delighted to score a point.

'The oï-stères were truly divine.'

During supper Edith spent a lot of time talking to Gary. She was very animated. They had an absolutely fascinating conversation about New York, about 'in' galleries, about 'in' restaurants, about California and, if this wasn't bad enough, they then started talking about skiing. They both adored the *hors piste*. How remarkable. And where do you ski? In Colorado? How wonderful. I can just see him, this bandanna'ed beanpole with his fluo anorak, his pink lip-sore cream and his streamlined Ray-Bans. I'd hang the bugger to the ski-lift like a Christmas turkey and press the button. Why are the French so infatuated with America?

A sudden ray of hope. Edith stood with the kind of smile that would open an oyster at fifteen yards.

'And for the dessert, I have little surprise.'

Clever girl. Wink wink. It's the secret message I've been waiting for. And I'm receiving you loud and clear. It's *libertinage* time.

'I have prepared a little Anglo-Saxon sweet.'

The guests are delighted.

''Ow lovely.'

'A puddingue.'

'Great!'

Haha. The crumble moment has arrived. I am about to stand when something terrible occurs. Gary, the oyster's friend, stands and takes my sun.

'*Je vous donne un coouuuuu du main?*'

Edith can say nothing. She is – at least I trust she is – victim of her own ruse. She is condemned to head off to the kitchen with this boring laid-back sky-scraper when she could have been in there rubbing her fingers against mine under the cake dish. She manages to hide her disappointment. It is so kind of him.

'It's nothing, Edith.'

And all the guests go overboard about his 'th'. 'Ediitthth-thththth'. They love trying to pronounce 'th' like Gary. They press their tongues against their front teeth and they splutter all over the table. I've got to find a way out of this situation. I start to collect up the plates with the idea of taking them back to the kitchen but the de Souza clone snatches them

from my hands. She's just dished them out. They're clean.
I go into terminal depression. Their mindless conversation
washes over me like froth over granite.

The crumble was shit.

Bad night. I had a dream.

'Edith,' he whispered, 'we must talk.'

'We must, my darling,' she whispered back, her hair
blowing in the strengthening wind.

'Tomorrow at six at the lighthouse.'

'Without fail, *mon cornichon*.'

The next morning he rose early. The storm filled the ocean
air with the bitter smell of seaweed and elastoplast. He thrust
two balls of cut loaf into each nostril to withstand the wind
and set off.

I woke up late. I could hear voices downstairs planning the
day in advance without me. The chums are all back again.
This is worse than the Club Med. Is there no privacy?

'Great, man!'

Harrison Ford was still there. He had slept in the garden
in his sleeping bag under the trees and the protective eye
of the squirrels – *les écouuuuuuuuuuuurueils*. Had I known
I would have slipped them something to give them instant
diarrhoea. I dressed quickly and arrived downstairs just as
everyone is leaving. No time for breakfast. What the hell's
going on? What's the rush? We're all off to '*faire le courant*'.
At a particular time of year when the tide goes out there is a
very strong current. All you have to do is to immerse yourself
in the long inroad the sea has made on the beach – a kind of
natural canal – and allow yourself to be swept out towards
the sea at some 20 kilometres an hour. *Le pied*.

Still soft from sleep, I have to jump on the emasculator
and leave for the beach. The men are in bathing costumes,
flaunting their *tablette de chocolat* – the muscles of the solar
plexus – which only self-discipline and a private gymnast,
two luxuries I have always shunned, can afford. They all

pedal very fast and race with each other. When Edith's chain comes off they are all too far ahead to hear her.

'*Attendez!*'

That is, apart from me.

At last we are alone together. I have been waiting for this moment for so long. I am also in the ideal position. Kneeling before her to attempt to put the chain back on I am perfectly placed to say what I have to say. I want to declare my love. I had time to work on my declaration all night. I cut, reshaped, added, refined. It is now ready. My pen and my heart are in unison. This is what I have to say.

'Edith, you are for me the incarnation of the French woman. You are all I have ever wanted. You are Madame Bovary. You are Phèdre. You are Manon Lescaut. Yes, you are fickle. Yes, you are difficult. Yes, you are quicksilver between my fingers. But you are at the same time exciting and dangerous. You are exacting, seductive, designing. You are all that the English aren't. I love your words, your language, your tenses, your agreements, your past participles, your subjunctives, your past anteriors. But above all I love your *liaisons*. I want to continue to be your pupil. I am not ready. I must repeat the year. Let me stay on. My education is not complete.'

The tenor of this declaration was, I will admit, at once stiff and over the top. But it has the advantage of combining passion and naïvety. I am sure that Edith would have been moved by it.

But I will never know.

At that precise moment, just as I was kneeling before her, a seagull, an ancient Greek seagull, a seagull straight out of Aeschylus, a long-beaked evil-eyed bird remote-controlled by some malicious divinity, shat on my head with the laser-like precision of a Tomahawk missile.

Schlouppfff.

Edith was in hysterics. She laughed so much she cried. She found me adorable kneeling before her with this celestial pancake on my head. She had never met anyone like me. The English are so wonderful. It could only happen to them. A lesson. There's nothing like a seagull with gutrot for restoring a passion on the wane. The others had turned round and come back to find out what was up. Gary, who, it transpired, had spent a summer as a mechanic on the route 66, mended the chain in a jiffy and my opportunity was lost for ever.

We hurried to the beach where groups of 'currentists' were already gathered. The men do a round of *baise-main* in their bathers. I see others in the distance doing it in rockpools. We all converged on a kind of giant jacuzzi into which we slipped and immersed ourselves waiting for the tide to turn.

'*C'est pour 11.03?*'

'*J'ai vu Dodo hier soir chez Claude-Henri. Elle m'a dit 11.04.*'

Being up to your neck in seaweed doesn't impair the French art of conversation.

And suddenly it started to happen. You could feel the undertow of the current. It was incredibly strong. Everyone started to turn, to whirl, to be sucked down the length of the canal.

But not me.

Having no desire to be part of the social whirl after my frustrated declaration of undying love, I had kept myself apart from the crowd to one side of the jacuzzi. With the result that I was out of alignment with the flow of the current. The others were already miles away down the canal heading for the sea. I tried to throw myself into the stream but the tail of the current just whipped me round and threw me back where I had come from. Another go. In vain. I ended up in a dead-end pool full of nastily spiked mussels. A last attempt. Too late. Powercut. The flow had dwindled to a dribble. I can hear cries of delight coming from miles away down the canal. The Delluc houseparty must be halfway to the sea by now.

I clambered out of the pool and stared into the distance, shading my eyes against the sun. All I could make out were thousands of heads bobbing up and down in the water like corks. The current continued to whisk them away until I couldn't see them anymore. Was that Edith waving to me? No, it was a mother and her child. Was that curly head Gary being swept back to America? No. It was a dead jelly-fish.

I cycled back to the house. Carefully avoiding Roland Delluc who was sitting in a shady corner of the garden, I composed a farewell note to Edith.

Les courants changent, les sables sont mouvants, un chenal semble subitement nous séparer. Je te remercie pour tout. Je ne t'oublierai jamais. With my love, Michael.

'Currents change. The sands are shifting. A channel now separates us. Thank you for everything. I shall never forget you. With my love, Michael.'

I reread it. Stiff again but heartfelt. Delluc started to stir. Sad but free, I left.

28

Back in Paris I invite myself to dinner at La Coupole. *Faut pas se laisser aller!*

I drink a bottle of champagne at the flat and arrive at nine o'clock at exactly the same time as myself. We like to be punctual. We enter the restaurant arm-in-arm. About as many people as on the Place de l'Etoile and curiously this evening going round faster. Whoops. Beg your pardon. The colour scheme has changed. The velvet is now green and no longer red, but the decorated pillars are still there, which was a good thing because we occasionally need to get our bearings as to where we are because we're already a shade plastered, *n'est-ce pas*. The *garçon coupolien* wants to give us a table on the sidelines but no sir we're having none of that you want a rumpus I'll give you a rumpus he doesn't fancy one and so we get what we want, a table in the middle left in spitting distance of the cupula I'll have another go copulata *merde* big bowl itself, and in viewing distance of the stars who always sit in the upper right corner. What shall we have to start. We'll have a *tartare de thon* for a starter a *tartare* to say hello now that's quite hilarious, tata goodbye pity no one but myself to share the joke with and the *garçon coupolien* doesn't seem multilingual in the humour department plus a *kir royal* forgetting that normally we dont drink *apéritifs* as *plouc* as a *kir royal* but to show that we're not prejudiced we have two. The *tartare* is totally uncooked could this be Blue Tartare what a good title for a novel I write it on the tablecloth and so we order another starter a *gratin de morue* totally divine but as the cod is salty it blows a little thirst up. The Sancerre duly ordered strangely turns out to be a wine that drinks itself must be *autoconsommable* because would you believe it there it was and there it wasn't. Anyone seen my Sancerre. We have a butcher's under the table, under the green no-longer-red banquette, under the coat of my neighbour, under the skirt of the L. Casta lookalike he is sitting next to. What can have happened? We all find this a hoot. One solution. A bottle of something *non-autoconsommable garçon, s'il vous plaît*. A half? If you wish. Indeed *une fillette* should do the trick nicely and help us wash down a *steak au poivre* and a *gratin* ... Just a minute ... *Gratin* dolphin? Unlikely, *gratin* dauphin ... *Gratin delphinium* ... very difficult to pronounce *garçon* would you have an accompaniment which is easier to pronounce no not *frites* I can of course pronounce *frites FRITES* so there but not *frites* because *frites* recall the *Réveillon*, the *Réveillon* the furniture wax, the furniture wax the Ile de Ré, the Ile de Ré the sea, the sea Didier the fish, Didier the fish Dédé l'Asperge, Dédé l'Asperge the *rognons blancs*, the *rognons blancs* sex, sex, love and Edith Delluc. Hic! Excuse me good gracious I'm hiccuping in French do I go *atchoum* instead of tishoo when I sneeze I try to take some pepper off the top of the steak to push it up my nose to experiment but the steak keeps moving about the plate and all this running after the meat creates yet another thirst so we decide to wet our whistle with the one wine we never order because we can't pronounce it normally we say broo and stop but would you believe it tonight we can say it Brouilly we'd like a Brouilly we stand up and say it to the assembled company BROUILLY who applaud would you believe it the best way to pronounce French is to get pissed. We'll do it again if you like. *Chiche*. No. Not *chiche*. Oh dear the steak is cold must be all that running about the plate but the *garçon coupolien* brings me a camembert and second *fillette* must be twins which goes down pleasantly a camembert *frites* original and delicious. To end the evening's festivities we order *une omelette norvégienne* if we can afford it haha which is great fun even if you are no longer peckish because it is decorated with little Japanese parasols and if you prick the baked Alaska it deflates. I deflated mine and in this new, travelling, foldable guise offered it to my new neighbours composed of him: glasses; her: tight dress. Good lord! My luck is in. There he is. Gérard Depardieu in person, looking for all the world like Bob Scott from Abesbury off to the gents. I've always admired Bob Depardieu and an autograph would do nicely to start my collection. The gents are downstairs, the stairs being reasonably negotiable but the down presenting some problems never mind this meant that Gérard must have arrived sometime before me because he's not at the stalls but I'm no fool a star is going to pee in a cubicle and so I knock on the doors gently tapping and querulously asking Gérard are you in there in French of course *Gérard êtes-vous dedans* or something like that when a gentleman in a DJ from upstairs kindly leads me back to my table, to my bill and to the door. We manage to get home me and myself leaning on one another and climb the stairs arm-in-arm just like at the Comédie Française. We have had a wonderful evening and lay out on the bed and go straight off to sleep because we are completely *cuits, beurrés, ivres, saoûls, pétés, ronds, noirs.*

29

On the rue du Cherche-Midi everything is closing down for the summer holidays. Behind the glass doors and the metal grill of the bar opposite Le Balto a pair of brown velvet curtains, like some moth-ridden catafalque, hide the sad sight of stacked tables and chairs where once there was life. The blinds are down on most of the bakeries – it is as difficult to find a baguette as it is to buy aspirin on a Sunday – and a scribbled notice *Congés annuels* has been stuck to the window, hastily sellotaped to the glass at an angle while the family and dogs waited outside in a overloaded car. There is less choice *chez* Didier. From mid-morning on, the live crabs and *crevettes*, like middle-aged holiday-makers on the beach, flee the sun to seek the shade of the *arrière boutique* where they prefer the company of inert fish to the heat of the asphalt. I popped into Nicolas to buy a bottle of rosé and discovered that Francis has already left for his holidays. He has been replaced by two charming students but I don't know them, they don't know me and I buy in three minutes that which would normally take me three-quarters of an hour. No *badinage*, no *dégustation*. I was put out that Francis hadn't said goodbye but it is true, I am now so much part of the rue du Cherche-Midi that he must unconsciously think I'll be there when he gets back.

I saunter. You can now. Paris is suddenly for sauntering. *Je flâne*. I know that once back in Abesbury I shall dream of Paris. I can see myself now down the bottom of the garden as dusk draws in, dreaming of the very street in which I am sauntering, of my flat, of Dédé l'Asperge joking with a Dane sitting at my table, of Edith taking a blueberry pie out of the oven for Thanksgiving as Gary tells her the rules of baseball or Jerry *le curling*. Life is fickle.

I've started to pack. The windows of the flat are wide open but the electric buzz of Paris is now more relaxed. I open a bottle of white – lacking in thigh but with hips – and empty my *ravioli au prosciutto* from last week into a saucepan of boiling water. They've gone a bit brown at the edges but I'm finishing what's left over. Crust of parmesan hiding behind a ten-month old prune yoghurt. Last night I went to bed late. Saw an old Truffaut – *Domicile conjugal* – at the Champollion in the same cinema where I shared my angst with a donkey. I'm going to have to get used to seeing Paris on the screen. Into Swindon in the rain to get a glimpse of the 6th. Siesta.

Tomorrow I leave.

There is a florist's near the rue Gounod. I bought a bunch of tinkerbells and left them at the *loge* for Madame de Souza to say goodbye and thank you. The shutters of the fourth floor are irremediably closed, there is obviously no one in but I take the lift up to the flat to say *au revoir* to the smell of polish and the doormat. I ring the bell a last time. It rings through the empty cavernous flat, echoing deep in the springs of my floral *pontage canapé*.

A final *apéro* chez Dédé l'Asperge. Lucien joins us. Dédé is closing in a few days, Lucien in a week. Very few customers. Dédé spends his time emptying half-full bottles into half-empty bottles, cleaning the *cave*, reading his paper with his half-moon glasses while Gilberte prepares a *salade Balto* for four famished tourists. Lucien tells me of *ortolans*. Those tiny birds – protected of course (wink wink), that of course you can no longer get your hands on (ditto), that you eat by sucking their guts through their backside? Lucien is a great romantic.

Outside on the pavement in the warm pink sunset we

all kiss and hug. It has been a wonderful year. With real emotion I present my patriotic red, white and blue braces to the *Club des cinq*. In memory of me.

A last kiss and a pummel.

'*Il faut que tu reviennes, Monsieur Mike!*'

An English family passes us on the pavement.

'Mummy! Look! Men kissing each other.'

'Yes, darling. They're French.'

30

Bad weather in the channel.

The fast ferry service Dieppe–Newhaven isn't running. I have to go up to Calais.

I'm in an evil mood. The motorway is crowded. Articulated trucks trail a plumage of rain behind them, making driving hell. The port is hideous, soulless. I stand on the upper deck of the floating supermarket which calls itself a ship and survey the wasteland beneath me. Endless cars in lanes waiting for the next ferry in a desolate industrial no-man's-land. Rusty containers, ugly concrete bridges over railway lines invaded by weeds, arrows, signs, portakabins, dank echoing warehouses. On the quay directly below me a group of men in yellow fluorescent jackets are shouting down a walky-talky which is a *talkie-walkie* in French. Only this makes me smile. All the rest is hell.

I'm wrong to be in a bad mood. France is doing me one last favour. It dresses up ugly to attenuate the pain of leaving. Everything is *moche* – the weather, the port, the boat – all on purpose so that I won't feel bad.

But it can't fool me.

I love this country. I love the people, the language, the streets, the smells, the buses, the posters, the bread, the *saucissons*, the wine, the bars, the books, the ideas, the women, the pleasures, the friends. I love them all so much that what I don't like – the ridiculous infatuation with tall Americans – does nothing to attenuate my passion. But I have to go . . . home? The year is over. The page turned. You know what it is, man? It's *crou-el*, that's what it is. I don't want to go. I want to build a wall. I want the sailors to blockade the port. I want to take France with me. But no. I'm wrong. France must stay where she is, emerging prettily from the sea some twenty-odd miles off the coast of Britain, pp. 23–24 in the atlas on the scale one centimetre = ten kilometres. Some shed a tear for Hungary, Tasmania or Liechtenstein. For me, it's here.

La France est ma maîtresse.

The boat is leaving the dock. Bent double against the howling wind I walk back up the empty deck to stay close to the coastline which I don't want to leave and which, inexorably, is slipping away.

On Sundays I'll go to Dover with binoculars.

Envoi I: A French Lesson

I recently composed the following. It took me about ten days. I am very proud of it and have stuck a copy in the loo to be admired by all. I have also learned it off by heart and recite it while shaving:

Loin, bien loin au delà des toits et des flèches, comme la lueur d'un chaudron maléfique mitonné par des êtres d'un autre âge, le soleil commence sa tâche, chauffant, colorant, rosissant le gris crépusculaire de l'aube. Bientôt, dans une fanfare retentissante d'oranges, le disque céleste va entamer la ligne si nette de la démarcation entre le rêve et l'éveil. Déjà la ville, dans un demi-sommeil, commence à bouger, froissant ses draps, renversant un bidon de lait, toussant, s'étirant, se saluant. Et celui qui, ivre des affres de la création, sent vaciller son regard et peser ses paupières, l'artiste enfin, se prépare à la nuit du jour, après avoir vidé le jour nocturne de la création . . .

I am also chuffed with the translation, which took me a further week. I have likewise stuck it in the loo. This is what it means:

Far, far away, beyond the rooftops and spires, like an evil cauldron brewed by creatures from a past age, the sun begins its day, warming, colouring, tingeing with

pink the pre-drawn hues of grey. Soon, in a noisy fanfare of orange, the heavenly disc will break the frontier
between dream and reality. Already the town, only half
awake, begins to stir, creasing sheets, knocking over
milk churns, coughing, stretching, greeting. While he
who, drunk on the heady, painful joys of creation,
feels his gaze become heavy and his lids like lead –
let him be named – while the artist prepares himself
for the night of day, having emptied to the dregs the
nocturnal day of creation.

The only problem is that, however beautiful the French, the
subject-matter is a load of tripe. That's the problem with the
language. You get sidetracked by the pomp. I must attempt
to marry form and content. Remember: '*Il n'est strictement
impossible de céder à vos exigences, Albert*' merely comes
out as, 'No way, Bertie.'

Showing Off

The French are sticklers for correctness. If you don't get it
right, it's wrong and therefore unreadable or unlistenable to.
To compensate for an inevitably non-howler-proof performance, try slipping some classy variants into your French.
At least the ship sinks in style.

Two tips. Once a week – say every Thursday – use an
imperfect subjunctive. The Académie Française toyed with
the idea of making it redundant along with the circumflex
accent, but the French took to the streets. The imperfect
subjunctive is a complicated recipe requiring pencil, paper
and a neat vodka to perfect. At the same time, it is also
the form most likely to send goosebumps down your host's
spine. Limit yourself to the construction '*il aurait fallu que*'
which means 'I ought to have' and which is necessarily

followed by the imperfect subjunctive, e.g.: *il aurait fallu que j'arrivasse plus tôt* ('I ought to have come earlier') would ensure instant pardon for any late arrival. '*Il aurait fallu que je me méfiasse de ton coq au vin*' ('I should have been wary of your *coq au vin*') will compensate for inelegance if you find yourself farting after the stew.

Second tip: invert. Very classy. Don't say '*Vous avez l'heure, s'il vous plaît?*' Try '*Avez-vous l'heure, s'il vous plaît?*' Or '*Auriez-vous le temps de m'accorder une petite faveur?*' After an intro like that you can ask for whatever you like. Don't invert at the same time or on the same day as the imperfect subjunctive. Both at once is overdoing it. If the subjunctive is Thursday, invert, say, no later than Tuesday afternoon.

Glossary

When you learn a language, the number of words you ingurgitate is considerable. Take the average dictionary, imagine that each entry is detachable, then empty the book on to the floor. The following list is short. But it is a beginning, better than nothing, and could help you break the ice with someone next to you on the bus: 'Excuse me, but my livarot has burst its hernia belt.' You never know.

à l'aise Blaise: a hip(ish) expression – 'Things okay with you?' To which you will henceforth reply '*Ca roule Raoul*' – 'Things are fine'. Practise in the mirror. The reply is even more effective if you manufacture a false Boyard from a yellow tube of thin paper which you fill with straw and glue to your bottom lip. Prefer lip gloss to Uhu.
le bail: a lease. The plural is odd – *baux*. It's the same for garlic, *ail*, plural *aulx*, pronounced 'oh' as in 'Aulx dear I've eaten too much bloody garlic.' If this happens to be

the case try chewing raw parsley (*le persil* is not washing powder) if you find yourself within breathing distance of a handy patch.

une banane: a quiff, as in *Grease*. Also a sardonic way of referring to a broad smile. *Il avait une de ces bananes . . .*

le bief (see *laîche*): a useless word meaning mill race. If you ever happen to come across one drop something in it which will enable you to use the word.

bouffer: to eat. *Manger* is more elegant. *Se gaver* is to stuff your face. If you want to make people smile try *se taper la cloche* – imagine the head as a bell, and the knife and fork as clangers.

le brouillard: legends die hard. You'll still meet people who think that Britain is engulfed in fog which explains why no one has yet seen *le monstre du Lochness*. Be patient. Think how the French feel when you roll out the striped pully and the plaited onions.

la Bouillabaisse: a stew made with fish which used to flourish in the Mediterranean. Since the Mediterranean has been turned into a liquid dustbin they have doubtless been imported from fish farms in Greece and fed on flour made from ground-down battery chickens.

Bordel!: literally, 'Brothel!' A common exclamation of annoyance. '*Bordel! J'ai laissé tomber les clés de la bagnole dans le bief!*' Or, if you prefer, '*Putain!*' as in 'Brothel!/Whore! I've dropped the car keys in the mill race.'

une cantine: canteen. Very chic if used in connection with a smart restaurant: '*Bocuse? Mais c'est ma cantine . . .*'

Ca va-t'y?: how are you? The *t'y* adds a peasant tang to the greeting *Ca va?* The kind of French the Archers might use.

la chute des reins: 'small of the back' is too precise a translation and is only associated with rheumatism or tickling. The only other choice – 'kidneys' – is on the other hand only associated with boxing and crusty pies.

'*Quelle belle chute des reins . . .*' is difficult to render in English. 'What wonderful kidneys' is not quite as sexy.

un con: a fool or a bloody idiot. Times – and comedy with it – have changed. There was once *l'idiot* – the Fernandel figure – a dreamy simpleton with his heart in the right place. The *con* has recently taken his place – Jacques Villeret in *Le Dîner des cons* – less dreamy, more thick and stupid. But we're still on his side. The latest development is *le nul* – thick, stupid and venal.

une crémerie: a shop specialising in butter and milk products. It used to be a small restaurant. It still exists in the expression '*On s'emmerde; changeons de crémerie*' – let's go somewhere else.

l'éminence grise: a force behind the throne, originally used for Richelieu in his cardinal's robes. *Eminence* is also a famous brand of French Y-fronts but the term is not used to refer to elderly underpants.

un empêchement: a hitch. A very useful word. If you don't want to do something just have one: '*Désolé, j'ai eu un empêchement.*' It always works. The elegance of the euphemism and the implied request for discretion are such that no one will ask you for details.

ennui: a very elegant word for 'boredom'. In Baudelaire's nineteenth-century French it was *le spleen*. Nowadays boredom is normally expressed as a verb: *je m'emmerde*. You can also – if so wished – indicate fatigue or lassitude by brushing your right cheek in a downward movement with the back of the fingers of your right hand and saying at the same time: '*La barbe!*' ('The beard!')

l'esprit de l'escalier: a neat expression for the *bon mot* which strikes you when you're out on the street looking for where you parked the car.

un fagot: a faggot. Useful in the expression *une bouteille de derrière les fagots* – a bottle kept stored away waiting for a special occasion.

filer à l'anglaise: to take French leave – this is the kind of novel *connerie* that everyone round the table knows but you can still get away with if they're pissed.

un fonctionnaire: a civil servant. People employed by the state are *fonctionnaires*. They are envied for their job security, disliked for their uncivil manners and are often on strike.

frimer: to show off. But, when you come to think of it, not quite. Certainly not to boast (*se vanter*). *Frimer* is what you might do with the second glass at a cocktail party confronted with *une belle brunette*. You take a black-and-white life and colour a few frames.

les gens: you won't believe this but *gens*, 'people', is feminine when the adjective precedes and masculine when it follows: *Les vieilles gens étaient très heureux . . .*

immarcescible: adjective meaning that which will never fade or wrinkle, i.e., unchanging, eternal. A red-hot compliment: '*Vous êtes ce soir, Simone, d'une beauté immarcescible.*' You can bet your bottom dollar that Simone will be over the moon when she goes home and looks it up.

jouir: a word less cold than 'climax' and less vulgar than 'come'. The French often use the expression '*prendre son pied*' which is a baby's expression of ecstasy. '*Chéri(e) j'ai pris mon pied*' does not indicate either theft or illicit acrobatics.

la laîche: the name of the long sharp-edged leaf of a plant that grows in marshy waters, used as the strips around a Livarot. This is an example of the kind of useless word I can always remember. You go into a shop, you desperately need an elastic band, a pin or a digestion pill and all you can remember is a hernia belt for fat cheese. I recently bought a bag of biological compost made from *le carex* – the posh name for *laîche*. Alone in the garden I thrilled at my science.

le libertinage: precisely what I came to France to learn. (All

French words ending in -*age* are, incidentally, masculine, apart from the three pairs *image/page*; *plage/nage*; *cage/rage*.) *Libertinage* is very eighteenth-century; very Marivaux. Or Fragonard. Clever, unprincipled, hedonist, unfaithful, loving, devoted, detached. All this practised as an art. Uphill for congregationalists.

le look: meaning precisely what it says. Official bodies tend to legislate in vain on the non-appropriation of foreign words in French. *Jeune pousse* – which sounds like an unpromising Vietnamese film – was declared a translation of 'start-up'. The Minister of Culture in the Juppé government of the early 1990s, Monsieur Toubon, made a bit of a *derrière de cochon* of himself by defending this activity. He did not, however, go as far as to drink a *Johnny Marcheur* or a *Marie saignante*.

louche: 'shady', 'suspicious-looking' as an adjective; the verb *loucher* means to squint; *une louche* is a ladle. You follow.

la maîtresse de maison: not a handy domestic arrangement but the lady who invites you to dinner. One can of course lead to another.

merci: 'thank you' – but be careful. If you are offered a dish at table *merci* means 'no, thank you'. *Je veux bien* will ensure more.

miam!: yummy! Onomatopoeia takes time to master. The French, for instance, go *atchoum!* when they sneeze and *plouf!* when they fall in a lake.

moule: when masculine, a mould as for making tarts. When feminine, a mussel. Careful what you order in restaurants. Likewise for *mousse*. Chocolate and frothy when feminine, a cabin boy when masculine. There is of course no accounting for taste.

plouc: a delightful adjective meaning 'unsophisticated'. 'You've never read——?' (Here you fill in the name of an author you haven't read either but have been meaning to for some time, e.g., Proust.) *Quel plouc!*

prendre un petit noir sur le zinc: nothing to do with politically incorrect sexual practices on the roof, merely an invitation to have an espresso at the bar.

public: state – therefore the opposite of public as in school: *une école publique* = a state school.

un sigle: an acronym. You can't understand French without them. *HLM* – a tower block; *BCBG* – a Sloane; *RPR* – the conservatives; *PS* – New Labour (although M. Jospin would not agree); *PACS* – the *pacte civil de solidarité*, the non-church, non-registry office, legally recognised marriage open to all couples. It has given birth to the verb *pacser*.

sur le pouce: to grab a bite to eat – literally, 'on the thumb'. There are a host of great figurative expressions in French: *poser un lapin* – 'to put a rabbit' – means to stand someone up. *Chercher midi à quatorze heures*: to look for the obvious far too late; *un pince fesse*: a cocktail party.

une tarte: a tart, but never metaphorically. *Une tarte dans les Bois de Boulogne* could thus ever only be construed as a bucolic picnic dessert.

le verlan: the form of slang rappers use. You take the last syllable and put it on the front of the word as a prefix. *Fête* becomes *teuf*; *réesoi* means *soirée*; *meuf* is *femme*; *keum* means *mec* (bloke). Don't overdo it.

une vespasienne: a public urinal, now replaced but still prominent in the national mythology. Named after the emperor Vespasian who apparently first equipped Rome with public loos. While we're on emperors, there is also *claudiquer* – to limp – because that's just what Claudius did. This kind of stuff is very useful with the nuts after dinner. *Néroner* doesn't exist and therefore doesn't mean fiddling in the flames.

Envoi II: The Recipes of the Famous Five

1. *Oreilles à la lyonnaise*

The best time to prepare this dish is in the late morning – ears can be knocked up for lunch – in a well-lit kitchen with the sun coming in through half-closed shutters. A glass of a cool Vouvray demi-sec and a CD of smoochy French hits from the past – for instance, Hervé Vilard singing 'Capri c'est fini' – are the other necessary ingredients. The Japanese would doubtless have played late Beethoven quartets to the pig in its last days but I wouldn't try requiring such niceties of the *charcutier*.

Buy ready cooked ears. You can of course cook them yourself but the *charcutier* has doubtless simmered them overnight in the vat with the *jambonneau* etc., and rubbing shoulders with the prime cuts will have done the appendages no harm.

Liberally pour olive oil into a thick-bottomed frying-pan. Not too much, but remember ears are sticky jobs and can leech themselves to the bottom in no time. Cut the ears into sturdy strips, taking care not to eat them as you cut them up otherwise you'll have nothing to cook. Throw them into the hot oil. Cook for about 5 minutes, all the time giving them a vigorous nudge with the wooden spoon so they won't stick or coagulate. Season. Toss them out on to a large, old, slightly chipped, previously warmed serving dish when they're crispish on the outside and soft in the middle. Pour a couple of glugs of good wine vinegar into the pan, scrape, twiddle and salivate (don't dribble into the sauce) and toss in a handful of roughly chopped chervil or flat parsley. Throw the ears back in for one last fling in the pan, all the while singing the overture to *Carousel*, and serve with charlotte potatoes cooked in their skins and a light, cool Chinon.

2. *Tripes à la mode de Caen*

For this recipe fresh tripe is required. Do not accept pre-cooked tripe, second-hand tripe, powdered tripe or inflatable tripe. We need the real thing. Take the opportunity of impressing the butcher with your tripe requirements: 250 grams of *gras double*, *bonnet*, *nid d'abeille*, *franche-mule* and *museau*. If the rosé has eaten into your grey matter, these names can be written on a piece of paper concealed in a hanky. This in French is called an *anti-sèche*.

Essentially this dish is a construction. In a heavy-bottomed pot you are going to build a house of tripe. The foundations? A calf's hoof, bones and all, which ultimately provides the gunge for holding the whole lot together. No calf, no gunge. And gungeless tripe is unacceptable.

Ground floor: a layer of rough-cut onions and carrots. Half and half. Second floor: tripe number one. The tripe should be cut into squares measuring about 4 cm square: metric tripe rulers are available in all good tripemongers. Third floor: more onions and carrots. Fourth floor: tripe number 2. And so on until you've reached the attic tripe. At which point you drench the construction in 20 decilitres of water to which you have added a dash of white wine. Then add salt and pepper. Coarse and sea, obviously. Nothing blanched or ground.

The next bit is fun. You put the heavy lid back on the pot and seal the edge with a thick pastry which is designed not to let the gunge out. This is very important; evaporating gunge can destroy the tripe effect. The pastry is made from

3 tablespoons of flour to 6 tablespoons of water. The fun is trying to get the sticky pastry off your fingers on to the rim. Friends can be called in.

The French call this pastry activity *luter*. With one 't'. *Lutter* with two means to struggle, which might be more appropriate. You then put the signed and sealed recipient in a low oven for some eight hours.

You must now be zen. All great tripistes are zen. Do not panic. Seepage is the name of the game. The different storeys are going to leak. The floors are going to cave in. The construction is going to melt as the *franche-mule* seeps into the *bonnet* and the *bonnet* into the *nid d'abeille*. Tripe fusion is going to take place. Allow it to do so in peace. People have been known to press their ear to the pot only to produce an unintentional version of recipe number one. So do not ruin your lobes needlessly.

The French call this process *cuisson* (cooking) *à l'étouffée*. The first 'é' is the modern French equivalent of the Renaissance 'es'. The word thus once was *estouffée*. And it is this root which, believe it or not, has over the centuries – 'Come up to my place for an *estouff*'; 'Not bloody *estouff* again!' – given us the word 'stew'.

Lost in an etymological dream, I once smelled burning, panicked, broke the seal, thereby losing two hours of precious gunge fumes, only to discover that the smoke was caused by a dirty oven. Ashamed, I had to recall my sticky friends for another pastry gangbang.

Tripe I have found responds well to Romantic music. For *tripes à la mode de Caen* I would recommend *La Symphonie fantastique* by Berlioz. Serve either with *une marmelade d'échalotes* – shallots reduced in white wine with a slug of calva, or, if the object of the tripe festival is to seduce the love of your life, with a salad of raw truffles to which you will have added a dash of lemon and olive oil. This is very expensive but very effective. Take care. The erotic potential of tripe has long been overlooked.

3. Trotters *à la Sainte-Ménéhould*

Ingedients: trotters, a razor blade, bandages, a *court bouillon*, an alarm clock. First choose your trotters from a reputable trotter merchant. There are those who claim to prefer left to right or front to back, but in the trotter fraternity this is generally considered as showing off. Ensure that the trotters are not hairy. If by any chance they have anything coarser than a five o'clock shadow give them a quick shave. A sharp knife or a razor will do the trick. Tweezers would be unnecessarily loving; the recipe takes long enough as it is. Do not use Gillette shaving foam; this would adulterate the taste.

When you have a smooth trotter – and you might as well do as many as you can at once because the gas/electricity bill is going to be pretty steep (some people come into an arrangement with their bank before attempting trotters) – you then encase it mummy-fashion in a tightly rolled, toughish linen bandage. Prior first-aid experience is useful. The object of this exercise is to keep the trotter intact during the cooking because it has been known for the trotter and hence the cook to go to pieces during the process.

You have previously prepared a dense-ish *court bouillon* – for each litre of water two carrots, an onion, thyme, bay-leaf, parsley, salt, pepper and a dash of white wine just in case. You then immerse the mummified trotters in the *court bouillon* and cook them for forty hours.

I repeat, forty hours.

This means that if you are having people for a trotter bash on Saturday the latest immersion time is four o'clock on the Friday morning. Set the alarm and be prepared to face bandaged pork in the garish pre-dawn light of the kitchen neon. Take care to maintain a steady temperature throughout and make sure the *court bouillon* doesn't evaporate. In the meantime you can listen to the Complete Symphonies of Anton Bruckner and write your first novel.

Once the trotters have been cooked, allow them to cool in their juices and then extract them carefully from the *court bouillon* on a slatted spoon. Put the lot in the fridge – taking great care to calm the advances of the dog whose greedy intervention at this juncture, after forty hours of labour, would doubtless result in severe wounding and/or death.

Once the trotters are cold, remove the bandages – avoiding the Pavlovian British temptation to apply Germoline.

Your trotters are now ready and – the master stroke – can be eaten whole. Bones and all. Yes sir. From ankle to toenail you can consume the lot. Rub them gently with butter – like a football coach nursing a bruised muscle – roll them in beadcrumbs – *la chapelure* – and grill them. Serve with a purée of charlottes, a crisp green garlic salad and a velvety Rasteau.

You will, yes, be tired after this intense labour of love. I have known men whose heads have lovingly dropped only to come to rest on a delicious pillow of unctuous pork. Prior training is recommended. A week in the Bahamas in the run-up period helps, but of course puts up the price of the dish.

4. *Tête de veau*

In order to enjoy this delicious traditional French dish, two things are essential: 1. You must never look at it; 2. You must forget what it is. If you manage to obey these two vital strictures, the gates of paradise will open before you.

Some hints. Wear shades when you go to the butcher's to buy your rolled veal's head. This ruse causes no problems in summer, indeed you will look quite fashionable. In the winter, the sunglasses are slightly more mannered and I usually plump for the 'pink eye' solution ('*J'ai un petit problème avec mes yeux . . . La conjonctivite probablement . . .*' goes down very well). If you develop a passion for *tête de veau* and have to go back for the stuff twice a week, the permanence of pink eye and sunglasses will eventually raise fears of blindness. In this case switch butchers.

The *tête de veau* cooks for some two hours in a gently gurgling *court bouillon* to which you have added a dash of vinegar. Place the rolled head in the pot still wearing the glasses. *Attention!* At this juncture you run the danger of proximity. If the glass of the spectacles is thin – then squint. When squinting, however, take care not to miss the pot. A rolled veal's head can travel very fast over a tiled floor (circa 15 kph). Diving to save this slimy grey rugby ball from the clutches of an unsqueamish domestic animal results in an intimacy with the offal which defeats the point of wearing the sunglasses in the first place.

Remove the sunglasses. Prepare the *sauce gribiche*. This part of the process can be conducted without protection. A *gribiche* is knocked up from the yolk of a hardboiled egg beaten with capers, gherkins, flat parsley and olive oil. Take the opportunity of having a good look at the *gribiche* as it takes shape. You've not seen anything since the beginning of the morning and might feel a little bored.

The *tête de veau* must now be tested as to whether it is cooked. Put the sunglasses back on. The traditional method is the skewer, kebab or knitting needle (from which you will have previously removed the pullover). The needle has to be plunged into the head, rather like a drill in the earth's surface, and travel all the way through to the other side, meeting different textures of resistance on its way down: elastic skin, soft meat, thick tongue and, worst of all, the kind of dense gelatinous matter you associate with ectoplasm in sci-fi B-movies. The trick here is put into operation the 'concentration displacement faculty'. Think of something else. Either something totally unrelated – angels, sex or Bartok's string quartets – or, on the other hand, something related but pleasant – a haggis or someone you hate.

Remove the head and serve.

Carve by braille. Do not listen to the slurping sound when you cut the string holding all in place and the head unrolls on to the dish. Do not faint.

You have succeed in preparing it. You must now eat it. I have found that the best method of ingestion is to conduct a loud conversation about something you're passionately interested in – angels, sex, etc. Or to sit dangerously on the edge of your chair so that you have constantly to redress the balance. It is of course essential not to concentrate on what is in your mouth. You can naturally concentrate on the *sauce gribiche* – taking care, incidentally, if you are still wearing sunglasses not to put the *gribiche* on your flies.

The ultimate satisfaction afforded by this dish can be immense.

Whatever you do, don't think of babies.

Bon appétit.